LEADERSHIP CHRONICLES
—— *of a* ——
CORPORATE SAGE

FIVE KEYS TO BECOMING A MORE EFFECTIVE LEADER

SUSAN J. BETHANIS, EdD

KAPLAN)

PUBLISHING

New York

This publication is designed to provide accurate and authoritative information in regard to the subject matter covered. It is sold with the understanding that the publisher is not engaged in rendering legal, accounting, or other professional service. If legal advice or other expert assistance is required, the services of a competent professional person should be sought.

Acquisitions Editor: Jonathan Malysiak
Senior Managing Editor: Jack Kiburz
Interior Design: Lucy Jenkins
Cover Design: Design Solutions
Typesetting: Elizabeth Pitts

ITM Coaching is a trademark of Mariposa Leadership, Inc.

Published by Kaplan Publishing

Printed in the United States of America

07 08 09 10 9 8 7 6 5 4 3

Library of Congress Cataloging-in-Publication Data

Bethanis, Susan J.
    Leadership chronicles of a corporate sage: five keys to becoming a more effective leader / Susan J. Bethanis.
        p. cm.
    Includes bibliographical references.
    ISBN 0-7931-8603-X (5 × 7.375 hardcover)
1. Leadership. 2. Executive ability. 3. Executives—Training of. I. Title.
HD57.7.B48   2004
658.4′092—dc22   2004006174

Kaplan Publishing books are available at special quantity discounts to use for sales promotions, employee premiums, or educational purposes. Please email our Special Sales Department to order or for more information at kaplanpublishing@kaplan.com, or write to Kaplan Publishing, 1 Liberty Plaza, 24th Floor, New York, NY 10006.

Praise for *Leadership Chronicles of a Corporate Sage*

"A must-read book! *Leadership Chronicles of a Corporate Sage* provides critical insight for anyone in a leadership position."
MARK TONNESEN, VP, Information Technology, Cisco Systems

"If you read one leadership book this year, read *Leadership Chronicles of a Corporate Sage*. Not only will you get realistic insight into what executive coaching is all about, you also will learn useful skills and insights you can put into action right away."
JEFFREY JONES, SVP, Product Development & Management,
Washington Mutual

"Clever and compact! It offers all leaders, not just executives, timely and relevant advice in a refreshing way."
CHRIS WILLIAMS, VP, Human Resources, Yahoo!

"I highly recommend *Leadership Chronicles of a Corporate Sage* to any leader who is passionate about building a high performance team and inspiring the next generation of leaders who will follow in his/her footsteps."
MICHAEL HAKKERT, Director, Corporate Communications,
Veritas Software Corp.

"A straightforward and practical approach! *Leadership Chronicles of a Corporate Sage* takes complex concepts and turns them into commonsense applications through a real-life story. No matter what level of leader you are, the tools and references are worth the price of the book alone."
LUCY CARRICO, VP, Corporate Marketing, Charles Schwab & Co.

"*Leadership Chronicles of a Corporate Sage* is the inside scoop on executive coaching—the first book of its kind to take the mystery out of the process. A must-read for leaders who want to know if coaching is a fit for them. It's a huge contribution to the disciplines of coaching and leadership."
JEN HERRLINGER, Associate Director, Learning and Development, Scios Inc. (a J&J Company)

"*Leadership Chronicles of a Corporate Sage* is especially useful for the commanding, overwhelmed business leader struggling to do more in less time with less stress."
KRISTIN COBBLE, Organization Development Consultant, Gap Inc.

"Finally a book that shows us executive coaching in action. I will be using *Leadership Chronicles of a Corporate Sage* with both my executive coaching clients and my human resources students transitioning into executive coaching. It's straight-forward and 'de-myth-ifying'!"
JEREMY ROBINSON, Dean, Executive Coach Academy

To my clients

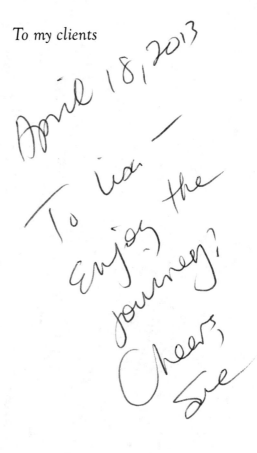

April 18, 2013

To lisa —

Enjoy the journey!

Cheers,
Sue

Contents

GO SLOW TO GO FAST
Leader as Learner

GET GOOD AT SMALL TALK
Leader as Relationship Builder

CRAFT A LEGACY WITH GREAT PEOPLE + VISION
Leader as Visionary

COACH IN-THE-MOMENT TO BUILD A LEGACY
Leader as Coach

ADD THE GLOBE
Leader as Globalist

Preface

I've written this book to give managers and executives a real-life, practical leadership guide that appeals to the curiosity in all of us. Max Sinclair—the semifictional leader in the book—could be your boss, your peer, or someone who works for you. Or, Max could be you. This book gives you an intimate view of one leader's reflections and struggles, which may be many of the same issues you face each week. This book also takes the mystery out of what happens in executive coaching.

You will be able to reflect on the same questions Max does and apply these lessons the next day at work. Through the eyes of his coach, you will see what Max resists, what he uses right away, and what he puts off. You will follow Max as he becomes a corporate sage. You also can read the book for pure entertainment. For fiction readers who just want to know what happens to Max over a six-month period, you will not be disappointed.

At the same time, it is important to acknowledge that I've written on a serious subject—the plight of one leader in the confounding world of American business and Silicon Valley. The emergence of wise leaders is imperative to corporations' sustainability. *Wise* means higher emotional intelligence, the ability to influence others for the common good, a long-lasting vision, coaching others instead of doing everything yourself, and a global perspective. These five key roles of the corporate sage—learner, relationship builder, visionary, coach, and globalist—are useful antidotes to a mentality of concern that has gripped many people in corporations. The events of 9/11 and political unrest have contributed to a rarely talked about crisis in meaning; Enron and other business fiascos have fueled the talk about lack of trust of managers; and the dot-com bubble burst has given way to a subconscious, dogged "waiting around for things to be the way they were" mentality. I don't believe there is going to be another modern-day gold rush. These days, I coach my clients to accept the "new normal," a state of being that necessitates an increase of skills and discernment, not stock options.

Here's what you can expect from this book:

- Listen in on coaching sessions over a six-month period and use these insights to prepare well for hiring an executive coach, if that is what you are thinking to do.
- The executive coach narrates this book dialogue. Sometimes, you will be privy to her inner dia-

logue, as she is deciding which way to take the conversation. This narrative will give you examples of the conscious adjustments that must be made when you coach others (whether you are a leader in an organization or a professional coach).

- The numerous skills and tools within the five key leadership roles that Max puts into practice are highlighted throughout the book and in a reference list at the end of the book. Use the questions to guide your thinking about becoming a corporate sage.

I welcome your comments and questions.

Sue Bethanis
San Francisco, May 2004
E-mail: sueb@mariposaleadership.com

Acknowledgments

Many people at Mariposa Leadership, Inc., contributed to this book. Thuy Sindell, director of client services, stuck by me end-to-end through conceptual development, a specific chapter-by-chapter outline, and final edits. More than anyone, she helped me breathe life into the book's dialogue. Reza Ahmadi, operations manager, gave me a much-needed steadiness throughout the writing process. Leadership coaches Janet Crawford and Alyssa Levy offered me their encouragement and valuable feedback on the manuscript.

Martha Jewett, my literary agent, has been a pure delight to work with, given her positive energy and commitment. Gerry Sindell, my book coach, shepherded me through the early stages and led me to Martha. Many thanks also to Jon Malysiak, acquisitions editor at Dearborn Trade, for believing in the power of this book.

This book couldn't exist without my clients. As a group, they are a constant source of inspiration to me, and they have been my teachers. I especially want to thank Chris Sinton for his unwavering commitment to the coaching-learning process and for providing me helpful insights on the manuscript.

I am grateful to Lucy Freedman and Lisa Marshall, who have influenced me significantly in the content and practice of communication skills—the core of being a corporate sage. Thanks also go to Kristin Cobble, who has shaped my thinking in the realm of organizational vision and legacy.

Other dear friends and colleagues who have inspired my writing are Dave Ancel, Julie Cotton, Jaye Flood, Ellen Herda, Leslie Katz, Bill McLawhon, Jeremy Robinson, Karen Seidman, Avis Stafford, and the "poker gals."

In the background consistently supporting me in my writing and career are my parents and brother, Joan, Jim, and Mark, and my extended family, Jeannine, Gale, Susie and Derek, Jeff, Ed and Flo, Michelle and Chris, and Lynnie and Melinda.

The kids in my life—Kristin, Amy, Dana, Carter, Kendall, William John, Kaelan, Wesley, Erin, Kendra, PJ, Taunti, and Ariella—have been a constant reminder of the utmost importance of crafting a legacy that lasts.

Finally, the most precious person in my life—my partner Susie Jordan—has given me unconditional love and support throughout the past two years, which helped me discover a newfound fluidity and ease in my ability to just sit down and write.

Introduction

Max Sinclair is the classic Silicon Valley leader: young, smart, and speedy. As a senior director at Solano Technologies, Max led his teams through the 1999 boom, the aftermath of 9/11, several rounds of layoffs, and a resurgence of the high-technology industry. Two months ago, in July, he was promoted to vice president of information technology (IT) of the 2,800-person software company, reporting directly to the chief operations officer.

Considered a "high-potential" employee because of his ability to problem solve and get things done, Max also showed a lack of leadership maturity at times. He was known for his impetuousness and for being hard on himself and others. His boss rewarded Max with the promotion with the caveat that he would work on his leadership skills.

After several conversations with Max and his boss, the vice president of human resources suggested to Max that working with an executive coach one-on-one over time would help him become a more well-rounded leader.

The HR VP gave me a call because she thought I would be a good match for Max's quick wit. He is a pace-setter and sets a high standard for his employees, she told me, and he is also critical of others—albeit often in a teasing kind of way—and frequently comes off as too intense. Not everyone can handle it, she reported, so he really needs to polish his edges. He is a relentless driver who gets things done. He works 60 to 80 hours a week and relies on hard work and analysis to solve problems.

She emphasized that Max is a brain trust Solano could not afford to lose, and that the investment in his leadership development was very important to the company.

Before I contacted Max, I not only took in all the information from the HR VP over several phone calls, I also researched the company's attributes and called a colleague familiar with Solano's corporate culture. She described it as highly results oriented, interrupt driven, and a fun place to work.

When I reached Max by phone a couple of days later, his energy was uplifting, intense, and self-assured. In our brief conversation he expressed optimism and caution. He told me he is interested in working with someone who has an outside perspective as long as he or she understood what it's like in high tech. He also said that he didn't want anything "touchy-feely"; he wanted something solid. Coaching is practical, I assured him; it's skill oriented and action focused. At the same time, I told him, coaching sessions offer the opportunity to stop and reflect on the wisdom you already have.

We agreed to meet in person later in the week, so that I could learn more about his work and goals, and he could learn more about the coaching process.

FIRST KEY

GO SLOW TO
GO FAST

Leader as Learner

CHAPTER

— 1 —

The Match

Max greeted me in his office with an immediate smile and firm handshake. I quickly looked around: one wall of glass allowed him to look out to the cubicles and see a hint of the trees that lined the parking lot; two computer screens; lots of books; and four pictures, including a signed poster of Michael Jordan.

The opening pleasantries were short, which seemed to suit Max just fine. I inquired about the poster, because I figured there was a good story about it. But knowing Max wanted to dive in, I quickly asked, "So Max, what fires have you already had to put out today?"

He smiled, with a nod of acknowledgment. "A couple, already, believe it or not."

"Tell me about them."

"The finance team is an unhappy client. We still are not on the same page regarding the IT requirements on this one project, so I had to call the finance VP."

"Do you typically step in like that?"

"Well, if I have to. It's usually to solve a problem that's been escalated to the top engineer."

"I ask because this gives me an idea of what you are up against—and what is important to you. It helps me understand your work world."

"You probably already have figured out that it's really fast paced around here. You've talked with the HR VP a couple of times, right? I told her that I needed a coach who could keep up with me."

I nodded and chuckled to myself, knowing that I'm often brought in to work with fast-and-furious executives. I looked up at Max and assured him, "I think we will be OK there."

Max seemed relieved and, sure enough, jumped in at warp speed. "So what am I getting myself into here? What happens? Do we meet every week or talk on the phone, or what?"

I quickly responded to keep up with his pace. "We'll probably meet mostly in person and sometimes touch base on the phone. Typically, I meet with clients once a week in person. This is the best way to build and sustain momentum."

He fired right back. "What do we talk about every week?"

"It varies and depends on two things: the leadership goals you set up and the in-the-moment issues every week that you want to explore."

Max smiled and said, "A goal like 'Stop being so demanding!'"

"Yes, the HR VP mentioned that. I think she used the words 'polish your edges a bit.' What does that mean to you, Max?"

"Is that what she told you, that I need to 'polish my edges'?" he asked, with an inquisitive look on his face.

I nodded.

"She and my boss think I'm too critical, too demanding, and that I need to change that," Max said, as he rolled his eyes.

"Is that what *you* think, Max?"

"To a certain extent, but you know, somebody's got to get the work done around here. I look at it more as that I set high standards for others," he remarked proudly.

I made notes to myself and said, "I assume you hold these same high standards for yourself, too, and that you are equally critical and demanding of yourself?"

Max nodded enthusiastically. "Absolutely, even more so."

"So what in all this do you want to change?"

Max contemplated the question. "I think I'm demanding because I am getting demands on me constantly. I'm overwhelmed with all that I have to do. I'm used to it, and thrive on it, but lately I've really been under the gun."

I made another note to myself to delve into what was behind the "overwhelm." For now, my goal was to facilitate a discussion on his goals. "Feeling less overwhelmed coupled with being less demanding would be a goal, let's say, three months from now."

"Well, I hope it doesn't take that long!" he said sarcastically.

"We'll do it in stages, of course. Feeling less overwhelmed, though, is one way you will know we accomplished something together, right?"

"Yeah."

I noted to myself that he finally agreed to something wholeheartedly. "What I mean by stages is you can change some things right away that might lead to being less overwhelmed. Like something very action oriented. Making clear requests of your direct reports will allow you to delegate better, for example, and could help you become less stressed. *That* you could do tomorrow."

Max stared at me, looking unconvinced. "You already have homework for me, to make requests, you said?"

"Yes, if you are up for it."

"So, you think making requests will help me feel less overwhelmed?"

"Yes, if they are clear requests. I think it's a first step. And it's an important skill to master right away." I sensed a shift in Max from resistance to slight curiosity, so I decided to build on it. "May I suggest something to try out?"

"OK, go for it. You don't have to ask me. Isn't that what you are supposed to do, make suggestions? That's why we've brought you in, right?"

"I like to ask to see if you are ready to hear it, actually."

"Let's just assume I can take whatever you tell me from here on out. I like it when people are direct with me. I can handle feedback."

I smiled at how Max equated strength with confidence, and I wondered if he could really "take" my questions, suggestions, and requests that tested his vulnerability. I also interpreted his last statement as a vote of confidence that he wants to work together.

"OK, my suggestion is actually in the form of a request."

"Go for it."

"In the next week, whenever you need something done—whether it's directed to your administrative assistant, a peer, or a direct report—ask yourself three *request-making* questions in order to be clear." I showed him the list.

Who? Who is the request directed to? In other words, who owns the action?

What? What are the specific conditions that need to be in place, so that you will be satisfied with the results?

When? What is the time attached to the request? When is it due?

Max said, "OK, who gets the request, what are the specifics, when do I need it by? Sounds simple enough."

"The questions are simple; forming a habit isn't so simple. Of the three questions, is there one that you tend to leave out sometimes?"

"Definitely the third one, the 'When?' I think the whole company is bad about that."

"Are you willing to focus on the questions, especially the When? part, in the next week?

"Yeah."

"Good, will you ask yourself these questions at least once a day until we meet again?"

Max nodded and responded sarcastically, "Only once a day? I better be able to manage that."

"So we have an agreement."

"Yeah, I can already tell that you are going to make me stick to my agreements. I guess I don't want to feel overwhelmed by homework, because the very point of making requests is to take the pressure off, right?"

"Yes, the rationale behind request making is that if you are clear up front, then there will be less mess later."

"I hope you are right." He responded at a noticeably slower pace. "What I do know is I think you can help me. You are straightforward. That's good. I want to understand more, though. You said we would be meeting once a week, right?"

"Yes, that's my standard practice. Once a week, in person, for six months. I'll check in with your boss and the HR VP now, at the midway point, and at the end, to get their feedback and to ensure we're all on the same page. It's important that they are involved, especially because they got you into this." I smiled.

"Understandable."

I shifted the conversation back to Max's overarching goals. "So what else do you want to work on in the next three months?"

"Definitely want to work on strategy. It's so hard to get to it, given all the fire drills."

"What do you do now regarding strategy?"

Max laughed out loud. "Not enough. Hardly anything with my team in terms of long-term goals, and I really want to be more involved with bigger business decisions with my peers. Right now, I'm seen as a great technology mind; I am innovative. I want to be more involved with the overall strategy of the organization."

I looked up from my note taking. "Got it. What else?"

Max paused for a moment. "Well, I definitely want to focus on my communications with my team. I want to be more organized in meetings, and more influential with my peers, too."

"Let me make sure I have all of this." I read it out loud as I wrote it down: "(1) Be less stressed and less demanding, (2) be more strategic and influential with peers, and (3) have better communications with team."

Max agreed, "Yeah, that sums it up."

"Now that we have the goals down, let's talk more about what coaching is, exactly."

"Good. I want to understand what we're going to do. I mean, are we just going to sit around and talk? I understand that soft skills are important and everything, but the idea of just lots of talk doesn't do it for me."

"No, no. As I've said, we will talk once a week to check in. There's a lot in between as well."

Max laughed. "Yeah, the homework."

"Let me give you an analogy. Do you go to the gym?"

Max smiled, "I belong to a gym."

"And do you go?"

"Yeah, I try to go at least once on the weekends. Play some racquetball with a friend of mine."

"Does playing once a week make you a better racquetball player?"

"No way, I think I'm getting worse. And I'm really sore on Sundays."

"What about weight training? Have you ever done that on a regular basis?"

"Yeah, in college; and about four years ago, I was really into it. I even had a trainer to keep me on track."

"Ah, good. How often did you work with your trainer?"

"Once a week."

"And in between times you did a bunch of repetitions on the various weight machines, right?"

Max interrupted the flow. "I see your point. You and I are going to meet once a week, but there is work I have to do in between." He started to look concerned.

I immediately responded to the look. "Yes, that's how it works. Some of the homework, or practices as I like to call them, is observing *yourself* so you can make adjustments—in your behavior or perspective. And some of the practices involve observing *others* and your impact on them."

"Got it," he said with a look of relief. "My concern was that it will take up more of my time to do the home-work—like in school, when you have to spend hours a night on it."

"No, no. It needs to be a part of your everyday routine. Max, in order to change, you have to practice. Just like in sports, practice is about slowing down to try out new 'stuff' in order to be faster and better in the game."

"Whoa. You are saying to 'Slow down to go fast'?"

"Yes, it's the crux of learning."

"You sound like you have been in athletics yourself."

"Yes, for 20 years: 10 as an athlete and 10 as a coach."

"Really, that's a long time. What did you coach?"

"College volleyball."

"That's cool. I was hooked on basketball," Max added.

"You played in college?"

"Yeah, for a small Division I school—Miami of Ohio."

"Yes, the tough-to-get-into liberal arts school."

Max nodded.

"How did you get into technology?"

"I majored in math and music. After undergrad, I got my master's degree in computer science."

"In Ohio?"

"No, that's when I came out to California. Did my graduate work at Cal."

I crossed my index fingers and raised them up in front of me, and grimaced.

Max looked perplexed, and then smiled. "Oh yeah, I read in your bio that you went to Stanford for your master's degree, right?"

I nodded and smiled broadly. "I promise I won't hold it against you that you are a Cal grad. So what jobs did you get after grad school?"

Max chuckled. "Do you want to see my résumé?"

"No, no. I'm just curious about how you got here. What path you took. We're doing that getting-to-know-you stuff."

"OK, at first I went to work in the financial industry within IT. That's where I really learned about information technology, and how important it was to serve customers. Of course, the customers were all the business units and the service folks within the companies I worked for. I wanted to jump into high tech, into a faster environment. I figured it would suit me more."

I nodded as he continued.

"I came to Solano five years ago as a director within IT. I got lucky when the chief information officer left a year after I got here. I had proven myself as credible, but I know there was some reluctance on the CEO's part to put me in a VP role at first. So they bumped me up to a senior director and I reported to the SVP of customer support for a while. Then, a couple of months ago, I got another promotion to VP, and now I report to the COO."

"Lots of movement in just a couple of years."

"Every year I keep proving myself, and, I have to say, I felt a little slammed by having to use a coach," he admitted.

"Why is that?"

"Well, it feels like there's something wrong with me. I mean, they have promoted me two times in a year."

"As I said before, they are really behind you. Many of the executives I work with in other companies are like you. High potential, great performers, and very smart. And they have a few things they need to work on; some are apparent, and some are blind spots."

"Yeah, I definitely want to work on my skills. In some respects, I just wish I would have come up with the idea to use a coach."

"I see. Well, let's go back a minute here. What do you feel slammed about?"

"I definitely don't want to disappoint, on the one hand. And on the other hand, I get great results, which speak for themselves."

"So what if you could get great results *and* not be so overwhelmed?"

"Yeah."

"And not overwhelm others so much?"

"Yeah. I want that. Is it really possible?" he asked with skepticism.

"That's why we're here," I responded confidently. "Next week, let's talk about your leadership goals in more detail. The more specific we can get, the better we can track results over the next six months."

"Got it."

"Other important issues will come up, too, that have little to do with your original goals. We will be able to 'replay' what happened in a meeting, for example, and examine it a bit. Then we can rehearse, or 'preplay,' a new practice or behavior that will help you the next time."

"You are really into the sports thing, with 'replay' and 'preplay.'"

"Well, you won't forget it, will you?"

"True." He paused. "We're not going to playact, are we? I mean, sit here and pretend?"

"No, no. We don't have to; you can rehearse the main points in your head and/or write them down, and then use me as a sounding board. And as a reality check."

"OK, that's good. I thought we were going to do those unrealistic, touchy-feely role-play things you do in training classes."

"No, don't worry. We'll have conversations that are relevant."

"Good," he replied with relief.

"What I also have found is that most of the learning is incremental, realistic learning. There will be an occasional big 'aha,' too." I smiled. "That's why it's important to meet once a week to check in."

"Yeah, I get that now. At first, it seemed like too much time, but now I get how it helps the consistency factor."

"And for one hour a week, you get to slow down. Slowing down for that hour and practicing will help you go faster later."

"Yeah, I admit, I think that will be good for me."

"Of course, the only hard part is scheduling our meetings. I promise I'll work that out with your administrative assistant. I'm going to try to get the same time and day every week so we can get a rhythm going."

I paused and looked at Max more intently. "It has been good to get to know you, and I'm looking forward to going into more depth next week. Oh, remember, the practice for the week . . ."

Max finished my sentence, "Requests: Who? What? When?, right?"

"Yes, it may help you to jot down a few notes on your PDA. Do you use the notepad function on it?" I asked.

"As 'high tech' as I am, I still carry around this old beat-up notebook to meetings to capture important action items."

"OK, use the notebook as a way to capture some of your requests, especially at the end of meetings, when there are usually action items."

"Got it, coach."

I smiled with him. "See you next week."

2

Direction

Max motioned for me to come into his office, even though he was finishing up a phone call. "That was the HR VP. I told her I want to go with you as my leadership coach. She's happy that I'm happy." Max paused and smirked. "Her words, not mine."

I smiled. "Well, I'm happy you are happy, too. How has the week been since I saw you last?"

"Good, nothing too perplexing or eventful. Not as crazy as usual, actually." Max paused. "Hey, one thing the HR VP asked me was how long we will be working together. Did we agree to six months? I can't remember."

"We actually discussed it, but did not come to a conclusion. Given what I know so far about what you want to accomplish, I think six months will suit you. I can write the agreement letter to reflect this. There is always an 'out' clause at the three-month mark, so if you are not satisfied at that point, we can stop there."

"Has anybody ever done that?"

I paused to recall ten years of clients. "No, nobody has bowed out at the three-month mark because they weren't satisfied. I use it more as a milestone to check in with HR and the boss. I'll get their feedback and give them a brief update. Realize, though, that our conversations every week are confidential. I'll not go to them on a regular basis and talk with them about our conversations."

"That's a relief."

"I will talk with them here at the beginning to get their input and feedback on your goals."

"That's fine. I'm especially curious to see what my boss has to say."

"Glad you brought that up. I want to schedule a meeting with him before our meeting next week so, hopefully, I'll be able to go over his feedback with you in our next session. Is that OK with you?"

"That's fine. Will you give him a copy of the agreement letter?"

"Yes, it will have goals, time line, fees, and a confidentiality statement."

"OK."

"I want to spend more time today diving into the specifics of the leadership goals you established last week. Before we do that, I have a few questions."

"Go for it."

"How did your request making go this week?

"The 'Who?' is easy; I already do that on a regular basis because we have drilled the idea of ownership into the culture. I think people are accountable; it's just that they are overwhelmed and things may get dropped."

"You are not alone in this. The key is to minimize how often that happens."

"That's why the 'What?' and the 'When?' are so valuable. After doing this exercise through the week, I realize how often I don't even address the 'What?' and 'When?' Just as I suspected, without the 'When?' tasks often just go into the black hole, and people forget about them."

"How is it working so far?"

"Some of the actions in meetings late last week have already been done. In all cases so far, I was completely satisfied with the documents I got."

"That's great."

"I realized that what frustrates me more than anything is the constant revisions we do. If I'm clearer up front, there is less 'back and forth' and unnecessary revisions."

"Your up-front clarity is the key. I know with my staff, sometimes I welcome the 'back and forth' to ensure they are on the right track. On occasion, I didn't see the finished product until the very end, and I would have preferred some course correction along the way."

"Guess it depends how big a project is."

"Definitely." I paused. "Are you ready to hear about another facet of request making?"

"Sure."

"Another aspect of request making is how we respond to requests." I showed Max information on various responses.

A simple "Yes"

A "No" and the rationale behind the "No"

An alternative—for example, "I can't get that done by Monday; does Tuesday work, instead?"

I asked, "Of the three, which one do you use most often?"

"Definitely, the 'Yes' response. Sometimes, I use the alternative. I rarely turn someone down. It depends a lot on who's asking."

"I'm wondering how often you say 'No,' especially to unreasonable requests."

" 'No' is not in my vocabulary. Nor do I believe 'No' is part of Solano's culture."

"I figured. But here is the rub: How often do you agree to do something—you say 'Yes'—and slip the deadline because of the overload of requests?"

"Actually, I rarely slip deadlines. The problem is that I'm here until 10 PM sometimes to get things done that I said I would do."

"Where are these requests coming from?"

"My peers in finance, HR, customer support, mostly. They want me to be involved in the implementation plans, and late at night . . . that's when I'm editing work produced by my direct reports that's going to my peers."

"Sounds like you are getting things done, but it's at a pretty high price."

"Definitely."

"Some of the issue is about managing the requesters' expectations, right?" With Max's nod, I continued, "And perhaps figuring out what to delegate without being too demanding would help?" Max nodded again and added, "I think we need to prioritize better. The problem is even finding the time to prioritize."

I realized this was a good start to the conversation I wanted to have about delving more deeply into Max's leadership goals. "Six months from now, you said you definitely wanted to feel less overwhelmed; more delegation as well as prioritization will help. Is there anything else that will help you with this overwhelmed feeling?"

Max shot back, "More help; more people to actually delegate to. I need a person who can deal with the prioritization of all these projects and demands. But I'm not sure how I'm going to get the head count."

"Max, don't worry about how it's going to work yet. Stick to what you want to see in the future."

"OK, I know I'm always looking at the gaps."

"I'm doing my best to pull you out of your default," I smiled and hesitated a moment. "I'm going to note here that we should talk about the need for an operations-type role at some point. For now, let's stay on the various long-term leadership goals you have."

"OK."

I retrieved the second item from the leadership goals list: more strategic and influential with peers. "How do you see yourself being more strategic six months from now?"

Without a moment's hesitation, Max responded, "I want to take the time to meet with peers more often, be with people instead of behind the computer. I want to have just thinking time. I want to be on my boss's calendar more often."

"Good. All these outcomes have time elements attached so we can measure your progress."

"You said you wanted to be more influential, too. What does that look like?"

Max smiled broadly. "People agreeing with me all the time . . . just kidding." He paused. "I want to be in on major company decisions."

"OK." I looked down at the last goal: better communications with team. "What do you see in six months regarding your team?"

"I should let up a little. Not be so critical, I guess. I want more one-on-ones with them. And our team meetings—we need to consistently hold them and they need to be more organized."

"Great, Max, we have set the direction for your personal leadership course!"

At the end of our coaching session, I thought to myself: Max knew where to go and he knew what he wanted as evidenced by the clarity and pace of the conversation. Like many executives, he just needed a little push as to *how* to do it.

CHAPTER

3

Support

Max popped his head out of his office and said, "I'm just finishing up a conference call; it will be just a couple of minutes." He added, "I'm really curious to hear what my boss had to say."

I sat down and a few minutes later, started giving Max the feedback. "He's very supportive, really wants you to succeed, and sees your contributions as vital to the company. This, you already know."

"Well, it's nice to hear it again, especially from my boss. It's not like he doles out compliments on a regular basis."

"Really, he seems like a pretty positive guy."

"Yeah, he is. He walks around a lot. Holds town meetings. He and I just don't meet that often; he is always in other meetings. I'm surprised you were able to get on his calendar."

"He happened to be available this morning. Guess I lucked out. Ready to hear what else he had to say?"

"Yep."

"He sees your strengths as: the ability to get things done, very reliable; and he likes that you know the business so well, despite being a tech guy."

"OK, what is the hard stuff? I'm waiting for the 'but.'"

"Well, first, he wants you to be more of a thought leader with your peers and show more 'executive presence.'"

"'Executive presence'? What the hell is that?"

I laughed out loud. "It's a slippery term. Think of it as executive *influence*. It's a term often used as a catchall for everything from charisma to wisdom to persuasion to how you dress."

"How I dress? Did he actually mention that?"

"No. I'm just giving you some commonly used definitions. I did ask him what he meant: He focused more on your exuberance. He does not mind your strong opinions; it's just that sometimes, he thinks your passion for what is right gets in the way of listening to others' ideas and, in turn, lessens your ability to influence."

"Did he give you any examples?" Max asked eagerly.

"Yes, he cited meetings with him and your peers, which is when he sees you the most. He said the CEO has said the same thing. Likes your ideas, likes your ability to blend technology with business. And sometimes you are too staunch. And you seem to get upset when people don't see it your way."

Max sighed, "I thought the big problem is that I am too demanding."

"That, too." Max looked frustrated so I stepped back. "Let's talk about that in a second. Describe what you think you are like in these meetings, the ones with the CEO and COO."

"I'm engaged and I definitely speak up a lot, but I would not say I get upset. I mean I don't feel upset."

"So you are giving off some perception that's not your intention?"

"Yeah, because honestly I don't feel upset in those meetings. They are all pretty professional. I have to say I've been upset in other situations."

"OK, I still want to go back to the senior staff meetings with your peers. Because here is where you really have to manage perceptions—which is a huge part of 'executive presence.' What exactly . . ."

Max interrupted, "Managing perceptions? That's manipulating. I'm a straight shooter. People will form their own opinions based on facts; you shouldn't have to manage their perceptions."

"Ideally you shouldn't," I agreed. "The reality is that if you don't effectively manage perceptions and align them with your actual intent, your facts won't be heard. Your ideas will fall on deaf ears if others have a negative preconceived notion of you."

Max gave in a little. "Maybe you're right, but I still don't think it should be that way."

"I understand." I paused a moment. "Let's take a closer look at this. It may even be that a simple shift would make a world of difference. Is that worth trying?"

"Sure."

"What exactly are you doing in these meetings that's creating a certain perception of you?"

"You mean like using my hands a lot, that kind of thing?"

"Yes. Any body language."

"Well, I usually stand up to make a point. I do use my hands a lot. Do you think that's it?"

"It could be. Are you pointing or putting your hands up?"

"Sometimes I point. Well, I probably point a lot. I do use my hands a lot, too."

"This could be intensifying things. So could your facial expressions. Perhaps a sigh or a dejected look. Your boss actually didn't mention your body language. He said it was mostly in your tone."

"My tone?" Max looked frustrated.

"Remember, this is about perception and regulating yourself. Your intentions may be great; it just may not look and sound like it."

"OK. I've heard this before. I just have to remember to control it."

"You're right. That's the hardest part. What will help remind you to take the edge off your tone and to cool it with the hand gestures?"

"I'm going to have to write myself a note."

"And what about in the heat of the meeting, when you are least likely to remember?" Max looked puzzled, and I decided to take a slightly different tack. I asked, "When things get heated up, and you are trying to make an important point, where does it hit you in your body?"

"Definitely in the chest. It tightens a bit."

"Good. That's your cue. When you feel that tightening, that's your cue to concentrate on your tone and hand gestures. Will you try this for the next week?"

"I'll try."

I sensed Max was not truly convinced. "Let's take a step back here. You need more of a rationale, don't you?"

"Yeah, I guess I need to understand why I'm doing this. Am I doing this just to please a couple of peers?"

"It's different from pleasing. It's about influencing. If your tone and gestures are overpowering, your peers may turn off. And you may lose your ability to use words to influence."

"Whatever happened to 'a good argument wins'?"

I smiled and said, "We Americans definitely have an advocacy culture, especially in Silicon Valley." I paused and wondered which way to guide the conversation, and decided it was a good time to challenge Max a bit. "Forget that your boss wants you to change for a second. Do you want be known as the guy who huffed and puffed his way to the top?"

"No. I just don't think it's *that* bad."

"I don't think it is either, based on the little I've seen and what your boss and the HR VP have said. I think it's a matter of catching it before it gets worse."

He smiled. "You may have a point there."

"I have another idea that would help you get more feedback on this and other matters."

Max smiled again. "Go for it!"

"Sometimes with the executives and managers I coach, I'll do eight to ten interviews with their peers and direct reports and put together a report."

"Do you want to do that with me?"

"Actually, I was thinking of something different. I think *you* should conduct the interviews instead. It will be a great way for you to build relationships and, at the same time, get great data from the people you interview."

"Is that normal? It sounds like it would be better if you did it," he said hesitantly.

"Yes, it's normal," I reassured him. "And no, I think it would be better if you did it. A couple of my clients have done it, with great results. You get firsthand what people think instead of hearing it through my filters. Plus, you become a model for the importance of getting feedback."

Max still looked concerned. "But do you think they will be honest with me?"

"Well, would you be honest if one of your colleagues came to you with a request for feedback?"

"Yeah. But I'm more direct than most people."

"Even if your colleagues are not direct about everything, you will still receive good information, and, most important, you will get to know them better. You can conduct the interviews now and then again in six or nine months to see the shifts in their responses."

"What the hell would I ask them?"

"Think about that and eight people you want to interview—a mixture of peers in information technology and other functions and a few of your direct reports. We can discuss this next week. Are you game for this?"

"I think so."

I sensed his hesitation and thought it was important to give him a head start. "Use your three leadership focus areas as a guide: (1) less stressed and less demanding, (2) more strategy and influence with peers, and (3) better communications with team. One question could be: 'I want to work on more strategic and cross-functional projects with you. Are things coming up that we could work on together?'"

Max nodded. "That's a good one."

"You could also get feedback about meetings by asking, 'What's your perception of my ability to collaborate in our senior staff meetings?'"

"I'll be interested in how that goes over."

"This is also a way to get info on how you and IT are perceived as a service group. You could ask about that, too."

Max's eyes widened. "Yeah, that makes a lot of sense. Kill two birds with one stone."

"Just one little piece of advice: Think of feedback as a gift, as a way of supporting you in your leadership path. I say this because I noticed something today in our conversation that will help you in your conversations with your peers and directs: A couple times when I was giving you feedback from your boss, you countered it, perhaps as a way to diffuse it. Do you know what I'm talking about?"

Max lowered his eyes. "Yep."

"When you are conducting the interviews, it will be good practice for you to just take in their comments, and

29

not defend or counter them. Just listen and write the comments down. Your tongue might be bleeding a bit, I realize."

I paused and looked back at my notes from my meeting with Max's boss. "I still have a few more things on my list from your boss, and we have a couple more minutes. Let me *gift* you with them." I looked up and smiled. "This would be a good time to practice listening and writing."

Max grabbed a pen.

"One of his biggest concerns is your team and succession planning. He is not sure if your direct report, the one that heads up IT for HR, is contributing all that he needs to be . . . he hears negative feedback from his clients."

Max started to speak, and then stopped himself.

I continued, "He is also concerned about your being overwhelmed. He described it as, 'You take on the world' a lot of the time. He thinks you need to let go of things and spend more time and energy on strategy."

Max wrote everything down in a methodical way, smiled broadly, and said, "Thanks for the feedback."

"You're welcome, and I'll see you next week."

4

Balance

I sat in Max's office for at least 20 minutes; his administrative assistant kept popping in to apologize that Max was running late from his last meeting. It gave me a chance to review past notes and to read again what I had planned to talk with Max about today.

Check in about:

1. Questions for his Leadership Skills Review—the interview process with peers and direct reports
2. Request-making process
3. How the feedback from his boss has sunk in
4. How focusing on tone and gestures has helped his influencing

When he finally arrived, Max looked flustered. "I almost canceled this week with you. It has been a crazy week. Been here until 10 PM every night."

"What's going on?"

"It's a network security issue. One of my teams is having a hard time tackling it."

"What's your role in it?"

"I'm dealing with a lot of unhappy VPs, trying to assure them that we're going to figure this one out quickly."

"Is that why you are here until 10 PM every night?"

"No, I'm doing the rest of my job from 6 to 10 PM, and dealing with the security issues during the day. I'm pretty beat."

"Understandably. How much more has to be done to resolve the issue?"

"That's the problem. Not sure yet."

"So you have been burning the midnight oil? In a good week, when do you usually get out of here?"

"I really try to get home no later than 8 PM. If I get home around 7 PM, then I usually log in from 10 PM to 12 AM to catch up on e-mail."

"Do you have a family?"

"Yep."

"How does this schedule sit with them?"

"It doesn't. My wife gets especially cranky when I miss dinner, which has been every day this week. My son and I sometimes hang out in the mornings for breakfast before he goes to school. And I try to spend one of the weekend days with him."

"How old is he?"

"Nine years old."

"That's great." I paused out of concern and wondered if this was a good time to call him on his torrid pace.

There seemed to be an opening. "Max, how long have you sustained this kind of pace?"

"I don't know. For a long time. I keep telling myself that this has got to change, but then crises happen like they did this week, which really set me back."

I nodded.

Max continued, "I do want more balance. I think I'm pushing my luck with my wife. Everyone is always talking about that work/life balance thing. Maybe I should think about it, too."

"What does your wife do?"

"She does marketing strategy; she's an independent consultant, so she has a lot more flexibility."

"Max, do you truly want to have more balance?"

"Yeah."

It was important to explore the depth of this commitment here. "What has stopped you so far?"

"Too much work. Not enough people to do the work. Too many unhappy internal customers. Escalations on the network."

"Remember last week when I mentioned what your boss said, about 'You taking on the world.' Do you see yourself that way?"

"No, I'm doing what is right. There's just a lot to do."

I wondered if Max really wanted to get to the bottom of this, or if he just wanted a quick fix. Both were needed. "Integrating" different aspects of our lives is more important than "balancing," when often something loses out. For now, I decided to go the easy route, knowing at some point we would look at this more deeply.

"Let's be practical for a moment here, Max. What do you think is a realistic goal in terms of spending more time with your family? Something you can measure."

Max thought for a moment: "To get home at 7 PM, and to only log on late, if I know there's a deadline pending. I shouldn't just log on to check e-mail."

I nodded. "I find checking e-mail just creates more work. What about the backlog of e-mail you are going to have in the morning that you didn't get to clear out the night before?"

"Yeah, that's definitely an issue."

"Can you schedule time in the morning when you get in that is blocked from any meetings?"

"No way. I get bombarded when I get in at 8 AM. I check voice mail on the way in, and there's usually something I have to take care of right away."

"Is there any time during the day that you could block just for 'e-mail time'?"

"It's tough. I would rather be with someone and solve a problem."

"Are you willing to get your administrative assistant to help you schedule e-mail time?"

"Yeah, because at this point, I'm really tired."

"OK, by next week, choose your e-mail time and let me know what it is."

I did not tell Max my ulterior motive. E-mail time will hopefully become "reflective time"—time to think through things, not just scurry through a ton of e-mail. Just getting time blocked out for something other than meetings was difficult. And this was a good start.

"Back to the network security issue. Is there anything more you want to say about it?"

Max and I spent the bulk of the session talking through various strategies for solving the network security issues, and with just ten more minutes, we still hadn't gotten to any of the original session goals. I thought it was important to spend a few minutes on what we had started in the past three weeks.

I said, "Given all this drama this week, did you have a chance to think about the questions you want to ask in your Leadership Skills Review interviews?"

"No way."

"OK. Let's just do them now."

"Yeah, but I'm concerned with when the hell I'm going to actually conduct these interviews."

"Don't try to do them all at once. Your administrative assistant can spread them over the next month, if necessary. Have you decided on the names so he can get started making the appointments?"

"Yep, got the names right here. I'll give them to him later this afternoon. I guess I should e-mail all the interviewees to let them know we're trying to get on their schedules."

I nodded. "Good, let's create the questions."

"I liked the ones you already gave me." Max rustled with the notes from the past week's session. "The ones about working with them on strategy and how they perceive me in meetings. And I really liked the service question."

"Let's choose a couple starter questions, as a way to ease into strategy. How about asking a general question about strengths and improvement areas as a communicator?"

"OK."

"What else do you want to know about yourself or about them?"

He paused. "I want to know how they find time to work on strategy."

We talked for a couple more minutes and came up with a great set of questions he would take to his colleagues.

What do you think my strengths are as a communicator? What do I need work on?

How do you find time in your day to work on strategy with your peers and with your team?

I want to work on more strategic and cross-functional projects with you. Are there things coming up that we could work on together?

What's your perception of my ability to collaborate in our staff meetings?

In what ways can my team and I serve your team better?

I looked down at my original list of goals for today's session. "One last thing: I want to check in about your request making. How is that coming along?"

"I'm glad you brought that up. I've been focusing on it pretty consistently, and what I realize is putting the 'When?' in is imperative, both when I am making requests and when I am responding to them. Having the time parameter expedites things; that's the good news."

"Great."

"But the bad news is that having the 'When?' associated with all these action items and requests exposes how much I and others slip deadlines. Sometimes, it just cannot be helped. What I want to know from you is: What have you found that has helped other executives communicate anticipated slippage?"

"What seems to work the best is a 'renegotiation' of the action and/or time needed. And the earlier you can go to the person and renegotiate, the better."

"Got it. I don't mind if people slip deadlines, I just want to know in advance what's going to happen so I can adjust accordingly."

"Exactly, and this is a great way to build credibility."

"Good point, especially right now. I have a few renegotiations I need to do. See you next week."

5

Slowing Down

Max waved me into his office and immediately said, "These interviews you are having me do, they are awfully interesting."

"Good, you've had a chance to start them."

"My assistant was able to schedule two since I saw you last. The first one with my client in finance was really good. I got a lot of good information."

"That's great!"

"No, wait, don't get too excited yet. I haven't told you about the second interview. That was with one of my peer's direct reports. It was like pulling teeth to get any info. It was hard."

"Was he distracted, or too tentative to give you information, or . . . ?"

Max interrupted, "He was suspicious. He didn't understand why in the world I would want to do these interviews."

"Had you sent him an e-mail to give him the background?"

"Oh yeah. I just think he was hesitant because nobody has done this before. He wanted to know how I was going to use the information. As we talked, I told him it was for my use only and that it was confidential."

"Did that ease his mind any?"

"Yeah, a little. But it was still hard. I think he didn't want to seem like he was tattling on people on my team. He eventually came around. Humor helped."

"Tell me what the interviewees had to say."

"The most interesting thing they said is that they see me as a 'cowboy-type'—one of them actually called me that."

"How did you take that?"

"I laughed because they laughed. One of them said he figured I knew that that was my reputation with people. Jeez, I don't even own any cowboy boots."

I started to match his sarcasm, and stopped myself. "What else did they say?"

"They both laughed out loud when I asked the collaboration question. They figured that you had put me up to that one."

"Was the laughter from uneasiness? Were they taking this seriously?"

"They're just not used to doing this sort of thing. We don't normally go around and ask these kinds of questions."

"How do you see it now? Did you end up actually getting some good ideas about how you could become a better collaborator?"

"At first when you suggested this, I was very hesitant. But now hearing their feedback firsthand has made an impact on me."

"What made an impact?"

"In so many words, I need to 'shut up.' Granted, they like that I'm full of ideas and that I solve problems on the spot."

"Did they say anything else about how they perceive you in meetings?"

"Sometimes I don't let others participate much and brainstorming is virtually nonexistent. They both referred to this. And one of them said I tend to look for the gaps a lot. That person attributed it to my computer-engineer mind-set."

Max seemed to have taken the feedback in stride. He showed me a side of him—some self-deprecation—that I hadn't seen before. I think he got a kick out of the way people characterized him. It seemed that Max was seeing some value in the process even though he had talked with only two people so far.

I responded to the "tend to look for gaps" comment. "Yes, I see what they are talking about. I've noticed that sometimes you do counter an idea before the idea has had time to bake. Bread needs time to rise, and people need time to think through things."

"Yeah, I'm not very patient. There are usually a ton of items we have to get through in a group meeting, for example, and we don't take the time to settle in."

I added, "What is probably contributing to this is that most people are not as speedy as you—in their thinking or their pace—so you may be leaving people in your wake."

Max scrunched up his face and seemed to be getting frustrated, "OK, I know I need to slow down. I don't want to leave people behind." He sighed, "But how do I do that and still get everything done?"

"The good news is that you want to slow down, you see the value in it. It takes self-monitoring to actually do it. Make things conscious, and you can change your behavior and change your attitude. But, first, you have to slow down and become conscious."

"OK, coach. I get it. And how the hell do I do this?"

"For the past four weeks, you *have* been doing this—slowing down to change behavior, using new simple actions like making a request with Who? What? When? and . . ."

Max finished my sentence, "That 'renegotiation' thing we talked about last week."

"Right. And remembering voice tone in senior staff meetings."

Max smiled. "And shutting up in senior staff meetings."

"Right. These are all about your conscious mind telling your body to change a habit that has been ingrained for a long time. There's also what is behind the behavior—your attitude—that includes perspectives, values, and motivation. Even if we change our behavior, eventually, our attitude has to catch up. Or, conversely, our attitude can give us the jump start we need to change."

"You are losing me. This sounds like a lot of psychobabble."

"It does not have to be. It's about fundamentals regarding learning and motivation. Think back to your sports days, Max. It was much easier to change your basketball habits if you believed it was important, not just because your coach told you to do something, right?"

"Yeah."

"And when you first learned a particular basketball move in practice—let's say posting down low, faking one way and going the other—you had to be conscious about making your body do each part of the move, right?"

"Right."

"Then eventually, in the game, you just thought about getting the ball in the hoop, not about the mechanics of posting down low, right?"

"Got it. So you're saying that learning a leadership skill is the same thing."

"Yes, it's just not as sweaty."

"Ha, ha. That was bad."

"Just trying to keep you on your toes. Don't want you to get too bored, Max."

"Our discussions are never boring, only challenging."

"I'll take that as a vote of confidence." I paused. "Back to slowing down, which, by the way, doesn't have to be boring. Do you want to know what's helped other leaders master this?"

Max smiled. "I'm all ears."

"As much as I don't like mechanistic metaphors, I still use this one because it's so useful. Think of five gear-shifts. If you compare yourself with others here at the company, what gear do you typically run on during the day at work?"

"Probably fourth gear."

"I agree with you, and when you are in crisis mode, you are probably running at five."

As usual, Max got the point quickly. "So, I should try to run on third gear more of the time? Not go so fast."

"Yes, running at fourth or fifth through typical city streets is dangerous, as a general rule," I smiled.

Max started to laugh and got distracted. "I keep thinking of when I was a kid, I used to watch that 'speed racer' show all the time. I wanted to be a speed racer."

"Let me bottom line it for you: You don't have to go slow or downshift all the time, just at the right times. Like when you are trying to learn a new skill, before you go into a meeting to remember to change your tone, when you are brainstorming with a group, when you . . ."

Max interrupted me in midsentence, "Need to re-member to shut up in meeting."

"Yes." I paused. "That one really got to you, didn't it? You have mentioned it a few times."

"Yeah, it stings a little."

"Are you in the right frame of mind to actually do something about it, to not interrupt so much in meetings?"

Max stopped. "Oh wow, I just did it with you, just interrupted, without realizing it."

I nodded and smiled, showing that I was glad that he caught himself. I paused for a moment longer. "Do you have more of these peer interview meetings on tap in the next week?"

Max whipped around in his chair to check his meeting schedule on his computer. "Yep, two on Friday."

"With . . . ?"

"With one of my direct reports and another internal customer, the marketing VP."

"Good, more chance to get feedback. Oh, and a chance to downshift to second gear. These interviews are good practice."

"Got it."

I got up, went to the door, looked back to say goodbye, and Max stopped me.

"Wait," he said as he motioned with his arms wildly. And then he didn't say anything. He hesitated some more and finally said with a soft voice, "With all this new stuff I'm learning, am I going to lose my edge?"

I came back to his desk, looked him straight in the eye, and said, "No, I promise you won't lose your edge. You are still you—smart, sassy, and speedy. You're just getting wiser, Max, and going slow to go fast."

SECOND KEY

GET GOOD AT
SMALL TALK

*Leader as
Relationship Builder*

6

Curiosity

Max greeted me with a burning question: "Why is it that the chats you and I have seem so easy, and when I'm doing these damn interviews it's really hard to get started?"

Normally, I like to craft a quick session agenda and ask a how-are-you question. But with Max, I flexed. It was better to pace him than to give him structure that he might resist. It was ironic that he asked about "hard starts" as he just launched in quickly with me.

I said, "You're saying it's hard to get started. Are you uncomfortable, are they, or . . . ?"

Max interrupted, "I told them about the process and went straight into the five interview questions, and it just seemed awkward."

"Is that what you normally do in meetings, launch into the agenda at hand? Or do you start with small talk?"

"I hate small talk. I've never been good at it. I just want to get into the meat of the problem. I'm actually known for that—jumping in and solving the problem."

"Yes, I have noticed in our meetings, you typically start with 'guns ablazing.' I'm personally fine with it, because you feel comfortable with it. Although, I can see how others might think you are a bit abrupt."

"Abrupt would be one way to describe me."

I slowed down my pace. "Max, do you want to get better at small talk?"

"You would have to give me a really good reason. It just seems like a waste of time." Max paused and then teased, "I mean I'm not that horrible. I smile and ask people how they are doing."

I lowered my eyes. "How admirable." Max seemed startled that I matched his sarcasm with a bit of my own.

He continued, "It's true. It's not like I just bolt in and out of meetings all the time."

"Just some of the time?"

"Well, yeah."

"I'm curious, what's the rush, usually?"

"I have places to go, people to see, you know, problems to solve."

"Are you saying you hardly ever just shoot the breeze with people to get to know them?"

"I take time to do that at staff meetings. I ask about people's families."

I paused a moment to reflect on my own assumptions because I didn't want to come off as too judgmental. "Max, I have to confess something. I'm a bit surprised.

I understand your impatience, but I figured your zest for learning might negate your need for speed. Tell me, on a scale of one to ten, how would you rate yourself on the 'curiosity scale.' One means you are not that curious, ten being very curious."

"It depends on what type of curiosity. I'm a ten when it comes to how things work and getting to what's behind a problem."

"What about when it comes to people?"

"Probably a six."

"Maybe you could associate curiosity with small talk to give it a positive spin."

"Never thought of it that way." He paused. "That still does not convince me that small talk is worth my time."

"Would some small talk have helped you get started on a comfortable note in your interviews this week?"

Max took a longer pause this time. "Perhaps."

"Small talk is vital in building relationships that, in turn, is the hallmark of influencing others. May I give you some ideas on small talk that go beyond weather, family, how's-your-day-going? type of conversations?"

"Go for it."

"Small talk is about rapport building. Anything you can do to get in sync with the other person is important. You can build rapport through body language, words, and tone, as well as by having good questions in your back pocket to get the conversation going."

"Well, I must have worn the wrong pants because I didn't have any questions in my back pocket. I could really use some."

I chuckled and showed Max a list of good *small talk* questions.

I haven't seen you, what have you been working on the past month?

Have you been traveling?

Have you talked with _____ (a colleague)?

What do you think of the new company _____ _____? (something you have in common)

Did you see that game last night?

I said, "Small talk is easier if you have done some homework. Find out what type of changes the person or his or her group have gone through and bring that up. Coming in curious and empathetic is key. I know you are empathetic with your customers. I've heard you. How can you be more empathetic with your employees and . . ."

Max interrupted, "These are all good questions, but this is really about making a decision. I just have to decide to take time to get to know people, pure and simple."

"OK, what could you have asked your colleagues in your interviews last Friday?"

"Because I had not seen either of them for a while, I could have asked them about their families, their plans for the weekend, what they are working on."

"What stopped you?"

"I was squeezed for time. I was late for both meetings, and in one case I had to hurry to a meeting afterward that was three buildings over."

"Is there anything else that got in the way?"

"I did not want to appear fake, and sometimes that preliminary stuff seems fake."

"I agree. It will seem fake if it's forced and 'techniquey.' That's why it's good to have a few *signature* questions—ones that feel comfortable to you—ready to go. Which of the ones we talked about do you relate to?"

"As I was reading through them, the one that made sense was 'What do you think of the new company's . . . ?' whatever, fill in the blank. With peers, I'll ask, 'What do you think of the COO's or CEO's decision on . . . ?' I also like to reference market and sales trends."

"Good."

"I also like to talk about sports with people I know like sports."

"Good. And what about with people who aren't into sports, or at least not into the sports you are into?"

"I think asking about traveling is good. Most people around here travel a lot, both for work and pleasure. And there are also a lot of people from other countries here."

"Great. The art of being curious goes both ways, so show your curiosity through questions and tone; let people be curious about you, too. Letting your guard down a bit with others and disclosing more of who you are will go a long way."

Max paused. "I let my guard down with you."

Before I spoke, I thought to myself, what a tender moment from such a tough guy. I smiled. "That's true." I took a deep breath. "Do I make it easier for you through my questions?"

Max went to his default and shot back, "Yeah, but you have not told me much about you—except that you were an athlete and a coach."

I chuckled to myself and realized he was right. I had not revealed much. "I am glad to share more of myself." I paused. "How about this? I read *People* magazine; I actually subscribe to it."

"Really?"

"Yes, I admit it. Seriously, is there anything you are interested in knowing about?"

"No, no, I'm just giving you a hard time."

"OK." I paused. "There's one more aspect of rapport building I want to share with you."

Max nodded.

"Not everyone is as speedy as you, right?"

"Right."

"It's possible to influence people more effectively by altering your voice tone or tempo so you are *matching* closer to theirs. So it's no surprise that probably 90 percent of the time, you will probably have to slow down your tempo. You will have to adjust because you talk really fast."

"What is this going to do, really?"

"The people you are with will most likely feel that you are really listening to them. That you are not blowing past them."

"OK."

"There's also body language. If the people are sitting, sit with them. If they are leaning back, lean back, too." I then adjusted my body position to match Max's exactly.

"This sounds like mimicking."

"No, it does not have to be. I mean, if you were adjusting every time somebody moved, it would look and feel bizarre. That's not what I'm suggesting; rather, it's most important not to be in a total 'mis-match.'"

"Mis-match?"

"Notice how we are sitting right now; we are both leaning back in our chairs." Then I changed my position. "Let's say I had my hands and elbows on your desk, leaning forward, trying to make a point. It feels different if I am way forward, doesn't it?"

"Actually, it does."

"Same thing if you were leaning forward, making a point." I motioned for him to change his position. "If I were way back in my chair, like this, you might interpret that I was not with you, and perhaps did not care."

"Hmm. Interesting. I think I do this matching thing already."

"You probably do, unconsciously. The key is to be more conscious of doing it, so you can be more consistent, and thus more effective." I paused for a moment, deliberating how best to get Max to apply this. "What interviews do you have coming up in the next week?"

Max said, "I think my assistant set up interviews with three people next Monday morning. One is my direct report, one is in charge of corporate strategy, and one is a business unit head."

"How are you going to prepare to build rapport this time?"

"The one guy—the head of the BU—is kind of like me. Cuts to the chase. He will have some good feedback for me. He is a big baseball fan, so I'll talk to him about the Giants game I went to last week."

"What about the voice tempo and tone?"

"He is actually from the South, so he has a slow drawl. He is a study in contrasts. Slow pace but very direct."

"So you will need to slow down to match him."

"Right."

Max scrunched up this face. "Doesn't this all seem a bit manipulative? All this planning ahead."

"I think it would be manipulative if your intentions were in the wrong place. But your goal is to get in sync, to hold a fruitful, effective conversation. Does that seem manipulative?"

"Probably not."

"What I propose," I smiled, "if you choose to accept, is for you to go into every meeting thinking about rapport building. Ask yourself these questions: (1) What one thing do I need to do to build common ground? (2) What one thing do I need to do to be in behavioral rapport? I showed him the summary of *rapport building*.

Match body language.

Match voice: tempo, tone.

Match language by asking questions using the other person's words.

Avoid mis-matching.

"What do you think?" I asked.

"I think it's easier for you than it will be for me."

"Ah, not true. It wasn't easy for me at first. Here is something about me that you don't know. While I've always been good at small talk—really since I was a little kid—I've had to force myself to learn to be in behavioral rapport with others. I used to miss cues all the time. I would talk way too fast and too loudly and would lose people from the get-go."

Max smiled. It seemed like he was glad that he wasn't the only one who loses people in the dust.

I continued, "Doesn't this sound familiar?"

"Yes."

"By the way, it has taken me years of practice to master this."

Max looked deflated. "Great, I have that to look forward to."

I laughed. "You are going to be better at this next week. Take things in increments." I paused. "So, Max, my proposal: Are you willing to think about those two questions before every meeting?"

"The 'build common ground, be in rapport' thing?"

"Remember it's behavioral rapport. Focus on the other person's behavior. Is he or she a fast talker, slow talker . . ."

He interrupted, "Got it." He paused and gave me a smirk. "OK, I'm willing to do it. But what about all the other homework you want me to do?"

"I know you have started to incorporate many tools. Don't worry about all the rest of them right now because you are already on your way. Just slow down and focus on the rapport building this week. We will talk about it next week."

"Got it. I'm actually kind of excited to try this out."

7

Networking

"How was your weekend?" Max asked me with enthusiastic eyes. We were meeting on a rare Monday afternoon, because he had to travel to the East Coast for the rest of the week.

"Good," I said. "I went to my favorite restaurant, Zuni Cafe, in the city. How was your weekend, Max?"

He seemed intent on making eye contact. "You won't believe it: I actually didn't look at my computer for the whole weekend."

"You took real time off. Great."

"Yep. I guess you're rubbing off on me."

"I'm glad." I smiled and paused, deciding where to take the conversation. "Didn't you have some of your interviews this morning?"

"Yeah, bright and early. Met the VP for corporate strategy for coffee at 7 AM."

"How did it go?"

"You mean, did I do the rapport thing?"

"Yes, that, and I'm curious what useful feedback you got. You have interviewed seven people so far, right?"

Max looked down at his folder and nodded.

Max began to answer my question. "My first meeting was awesome. We were definitely 'in sync'—your words," as he pointed to me. "He also asked me to work on a cross-functional assignment that the COO, who is over both of us, had asked him to head up. Normally, I'm too overloaded for these assignments; but this one is vital to the success of our company."

"What is it?"

"It's an online project management matrix for the whole company, so we can keep track of and adjust any and all company projects or initiatives. We can map them to our strategic goals and know what is going on in real time. It's really cool technology."

"Sounds like a great project to collaborate on—the project of projects. Tell me how you got in sync with him."

"His style is very different from mine, so I definitely thought about how to approach the meeting. I made sure that I went in more calm than usual, which wasn't so hard because I hadn't had my coffee yet. He's a strategist so he's more of a thinker type; he's kind of introverted."

"Does calm mean softer tone or slower tempo, or both?"

"Both."

"And did it work?"

"Yeah, coupled with some good starter questions. I've not seen him in a while, so I asked if he had been traveling at all. Turns out, he got back from Singapore just two weeks ago."

"Did he go for Solano?"

Max nodded. "He went there to talk to the head of the Asia-Pacific region."

"It sounds like you had a good conversation. Did you get any useful feedback?"

"Yeah. He gave me the thumbs-up for doing these interviews; he thought it was a great idea—a great 'networking technique' he called it."

"So a very different response from the first two interviewees."

"Oh yeah."

"You do get an added bonus with these interviews. You get feedback *and* you become better acquainted with people in the process. You never know when you will need to turn to these folks for something."

"I don't want to do interviews like this for the rest of my career," Max lamented.

"I understand that. Asking people for feedback on your personal skills and style is vulnerable. But some of the questions you are asking in these interviews are great networking questions, like how you can help them and how you can collaborate with them."

"OK."

"The interviews are giving you practice outside of your Information Technology group. This is vital to your new role as VP. You need to get to know people and they need to get to know you. You can turn these interviews into more informal conversations for the purposes of getting to know someone and gathering information."

"OK, got it."

"Also, remember our first meeting? One of your six-month leadership outcomes was that you want to be in on more company decisions. People will turn to you more often and get your input if you reach out to them on a regular basis."

"It's back to that time-sync again."

"Yes, I know. It's a trade-off. Spend more time now with people to prevent more problems in the future."

"That's so hard to do."

"Get your assistant to give you the discipline you need. Setting up the interviews was seamless to you; he did them all. Give him the action item to set up conversations with your peers and your boss's peers on a regular basis."

"What's the agenda in these conversations?"

"Focus on service and collaboration. Do at least two a month. And when you have talked with everyone, start over."

"Boy, you're tough."

I laughed. "I'm trying to be supportive, and sometimes, as a coach, I step into my consultant/mentor role. I've seen too many executives—new and seasoned—get burned."

"What do you mean: We, executives, get burned?"

"Thinking that what got you here is what is going to get you to the next level. Too many executives put their heads down and work their butts off in the same way they usually do. They think this hard work is going to lead to success."

"Ooh . . . that's ruthless."

"Yes, I'm on a roll. You were afforded the option to be the ultimate results-driven guy when you were a manager. As an executive, it's all about relationships." I put my hands up in front of me in an act of concession, and before he could remark, I said, "Max, I know I'm generalizing—just trying to make a point."

"OK, I'm with you. Truly, I'm starting to get it." He chuckled.

"Let me see, Max. Is your tongue in your cheek?"

"No, really. I believe you." He continued to chuckle, then paused. "I like when you get passionate."

"As long as it makes a difference to you."

"I guess I need to spend time networking. I will definitely get my assistant to help me. It would help to make a list of people right now, and then I'll just hand it to him."

After we spent a couple of minutes creating the list, I shifted to the week's work. "Tell me, what's on your agenda for your meetings in Boston?"

"My main meeting is with the general manager of one of our product groups. She is upset that our technology costs seem to be so much higher than if she were to go outside. I have to go and settle her down."

"OK, remember the rapport building."

"Got it. See you next Tuesday, right?"

I got up to leave. "Right."

8

Inquiry

Max's assistant popped his head into Max's office for the second time to tell me that Max was, indeed, on his way.

Ten minutes later, Max showed up with a wicked scowl on his face.

"What happened?" I asked. "You look really frustrated."

"I'm so pissed off at my boss. I just met with him and the head of corporate strategy. Remember that project I told you about last week?"

"Yes, the 'project of projects.'"

"I can't believe how much he is micromanaging on this thing. He gave it to us to handle, and now he wants to know our plan every step of the way."

"Do you know why he is micromanaging you?"

"Yeah, he's a control freak."

"Does he often micromanage you?"

"No."

"Again, do you know why he is micromanaging you on this one?"

"No."

"So you didn't ask about this—why he seemed to want to be so involved?"

"No, I just fought back."

"How so?"

"Well, he basically changed the direction of the project without getting input from us. And he wants to know our progress on a weekly basis—he never asked about weekly progress before. So I told him that I didn't agree with him on both accounts."

"Let's step back a second and take a look at his motivations. Why do you think he wants to be so involved?"

Max was still steaming, and I risked that this type of inquiry was going to fall flat or anger him more.

"I don't know. I guess maybe he is under pressure from his boss, the CEO."

"Bingo. Did that occur to you in the heat of the meeting?"

"No, I was too pissed off."

"Max, how will you know that the next time your blood is boiling you should 'get off the line'?"

"Get off the line? What the hell is that?"

"It's actually an aikido expression—it means to step away from the line of attack or resistance to see what is going on. In this case, getting off the line could translate into asking a question."

Max shook his head. "Easier said than done."

"Are you willing to try this when you are in a duel, so you can become more clearheaded?"

"I don't know actually. I'm not so sure in the heat of the moment I'll be able to just ask a question."

"What are you willing to do in the heat of the moment?"

"I don't know. Perhaps I need to just recognize that I am upset. I usually don't see it until it's too late."

"OK, will you focus on that, then?"

Max gave me his reluctant-looking nod. I paused a moment to give him time to switch gears. "Will you tell me how your meeting with the GM in Boston went?" I asked.

"That did not go so well, either."

"Seems like you have had a rough week since I saw you last."

"Yeah, I met with the GM twice, once in a team meeting with her and her direct reports, and in a one-on-one afterward. I presented a lot of persuasive data to show the tremendous cost savings they could have if they would continue with our internal IT team instead of going outside for the technology they need."

"The classic 'build or buy' dilemma."

Max tried to correct me, "Yes, but there was no dilemma, because we had the costs covered hands down. It seems like all that our CEO and COO have been preaching is cost cutting and being frugal."

"So what was the issue for her, then?"

"Well, she claims that I didn't spend any time on change management, that I just emphasized the product savings. That I didn't take into account the buy-in process—what it's going to take for people to really embrace this." He put his fingers up to feign quotations marks. "That was what she said, 'Embrace this.'"

"Does she have a point?"

"Well, yeah. But not enough to stall the start of the program."

"That's what she wants to do."

"Yeah."

"Who's the IT contact on this one? The one who got the original requirements? Did he or she not pick up that the change management aspect was one of her biggest concerns?"

"One of my guys dropped the ball, for sure. I know who it is now. I didn't know last week when I presented. My guy should have gotten that info from her guys."

"And they didn't tell you and you got hung out to dry." I paused. "So what happened in your one-on-one meeting with her after the team meeting?"

"Well, I had to deal with her being pissed off, and her going on and on about how she has told her staff of her concerns many times."

"You hadn't talked with her personally beforehand to make sure the two of you agreed on the requirements for this project?"

"No."

"As a standard practice, do you normally present to a team like that, without giving the leader of the team a heads up beforehand?"

"You know that we live and die with PowerPoint presentations."

"Yes, and that doesn't mean you don't give the GM a heads up, first."

Max shot back, "But that wastes time, when she is going to hear it anyway."

"Not if you have to have a one-on-one with her afterward to fix it. You could have saved yourself the headache by meeting with her beforehand to be sure she had bought into it."

"Well, what I didn't know is that the last IT VP sold her on a project that ended up failing miserably. And the main reason was people had never bought into it in the first place. She also expected a communication plan from me showing how this thing was to be integrated and everything."

"And when will you have this done?"

"I'm having one of my guys work on it as we speak."

"Let's step back a second and look at this thing, as well as at the meeting with your boss earlier this afternoon. Remember your goal—being more influential with peers and upper management. Here are two examples where you could have been more influential, right?"

"Yep."

"May I offer you some ideas?"

"Of course."

I handed Max information on *balancing inquiry and advocacy.*

Inquire: Before formal presentations and before you advocate a position, be sure you ask questions to understand what is important to the other person.

Know decision criteria: Understand the criteria the person will use to make a decision; know what motivates the other person. You may need to ask others who know the person how he or she makes decisions.

Advocate: Based on the other person's needs and requirements, develop your stance—be clear and let him or her know what your rationale is and how you came to your thinking.

Adjust: During formal presentations or one-on-ones, be aware when you need to adjust your inquiry or advocacy in order for a decision to be made.

I started to explain: "These distinctions are especially important when you are trying to persuade someone to make a decision. What do you think of the list? Evaluate yourself against it."

"I do a lot of advocacy, and I do ask a lot of questions, too. I often don't know the decision criteria, though. That's a good one."

"What about 'adjusting in the moment'?"

"So you want me to rate myself on how well I adjust? I nodded.

"Well, at this point I'm not that aware of it. What I do notice is if people need more info, I provide that."

"OK," I said. "Let's go back to the inquiry part. On question asking, where would you say, on a scale of one to ten, with interrogation being one and inquiry being ten, you fall?"

Max laughed. "Well, sometimes I do interrogate people when I ask them questions. I would say a five."

"OK, so in four months where would you like to be?"

"How about an eight?"

"OK, that's fair."

"I'm never going to be a ten. I'm just too intense."

I laughed and said, "You're probably right, and that's OK." I paused. "Let's talk about the decision criteria. It's very important to understand someone's motivation. In the case of the GM in Boston, for example, as it turns out, money was not the stumbling block. Adoption was."

"Yeah, probably should have gone to her beforehand."

"What would you have asked her to understand her decision criteria?"

"I would have asked 'What's in the way of the deal?'"

"That's a good question late in the game. What about early in the process when you are first meeting with her?"

"How about something simple like, 'What factors are going to be most important in your decision'?"

"Great. That will work well. And it can be applied in many situations."

"Got it."

I deliberated a moment about where to take the conversation. I thought it was best to give Max the opportunity to walk in another person's shoes. "I want to talk about another aspect of influencing that I think will help you out a lot: how 'influenceable' you are."

Max interrupted, "Wait a minute. 'Influenceable'? What the hell is that?"

"Hold on, Max, I was about to explain."

"OK, sorry. I interrupted you."

I nodded. "The more you are open to being influenced—your *influenceable factor*—the more likely you will be able to influence others. Let's use the same scale as before. One being not influenceable at all, and ten being influenceable, where do you stand?"

"I'm really stubborn, probably a two or three."

"OK, where do you want to get to?"

"Probably a six or seven. I mean, I don't want to be a milk toast and back down all the time."

"A ten isn't a milk toast. A ten means you are open to hearing others' points of view and welcome others' questions; it doesn't mean you cave."

"OK, I want to get to an eight, let's say, in four months."

"You are on. That's a good goal. Here's another way to look at it. You would rather be pulled through a dark room or a crowded concert than pushed, right?

"I would rather lead," Max laughed.

"Not if you didn't know the way and the other person did."

"Yeah, I guess."

"You would be more influential if you pulled people through a decision process than pushed them, right?"

"I'm with you."

"When you are influencing and being influenced, the skills of rapport building and using inquiry to understand the other person's point of view and the motivations behind his or her decision making are key—and just as important as having your data lined up and opinions well thought out."

Max pondered what I had to say and said slowly, "OK, rapport building and inquiry."

"Yes, your new best friends. Max, the best argument doesn't always win. But the best argument in the context of the other person's needs usually does. If you can master these skills, in combination with your quick ability to adjust and your competency in preparing comprehensive data for meetings, you will increase your ability to influence your peers a lot."

"Yet, again, you have figured out a way to influence me."

"I pulled you through it after you described situations where having these skills would have helped. You were ready to hear it—you have been open to me influencing you today. Your influenceable factor with me is quite high. Just think if your influenceable factor with others was as high."

"I don't trust others like I trust you."

I paused for a moment. "Thanks, Max."

"Well, it's true."

"Using rapport building and inquiry more can help others trust you, but it also helps you learn to trust them."

"I know, it's just hard to do." He paused and then lit up. "And I'm going to do it."

After two months of work, I think Max was ready to dig in and change like never before.

CRAFT A LEGACY WITH GREAT PEOPLE + VISION

Leader as Visionary

Great People

I was reading through last week's meeting notes in Max's office when he rushed in and told me that one of his direct reports—the IT director who works with the sales force—had quit out of the blue.

"What did he say?" I asked.

"He wrote me a damn e-mail over the weekend to let me know; we actually met yesterday. He said that he had a great opportunity at another company—and guess what, they just happen to be one of our big competitors."

"Did you have a chance to counteroffer or anything?"

"No, he was long gone; he didn't let me talk him out of it. Believe me, I tried to counteroffer."

"It didn't work?"

"Naw, he had his mind made up and had already accepted their offer."

"I'm curious: Before you countered his offer, did you ask him some questions to find out more about his decision for leaving?"

"You mean, did I use the rapport and inquiry stuff?"

Max made me laugh. "So you did remember."

"Yeah, in fact, I started to call you on the cell yesterday to help me prepare for this meeting and then I got sidetracked. So, instead, right before my meeting with him, I pretended to have a conversation with you as a way to prepare."

"Great."

"When I got into the meeting, I was very good about 'matching' him when he came into my office. I slowed down a lot, and really listened. I asked him a lot of questions, without interrogating him."

Even though he was reporting on success with his relationship-building skills, understandably, Max continued to look dejected. I thought it was important to give him a chance to talk about his feelings before we moved to a solution.

Max looked out the big office window to the cubicles. "I'm really bummed about this. He was my best guy."

"Totally understandable. I'm sorry, Max. It's hard to lose good people, especially if it's a surprise. Do you feel a little betrayed because he had not let on about it?"

"Yeah, sort of. I really thought he was happy here and that everything was going well. He said he was happy, but that this other opportunity was just too good to pass up."

"Do you believe him? I mean, did you ask him if there was anything going on here that contributed to his leaving?"

"He said that he was stressed out, but he didn't think that was going to change in another job, especially at the beginning. He also said something else that was hard to hear."

"What?"

"He said that things had just gotten too chaotic. We had grown wildly with no processes and procedures in place at the end of the 1990s. And then with the downturn and layoffs, there were fewer people to do the same amount of work. He also said there were just way too many pocket vetos."

"Pocket vetos?"

"You know, people agree to do something in a meeting and then veto the action to themselves after the meeting. They don't do the task, nor do they inform anyone that they are not doing it."

"Ah, I get it. Again, you seem surprised by this, too."

"Well, I thought things were getting better. Especially since I had been getting some feedback that the request-making skills were helping, that things were getting better on the team."

"He didn't think things were getting better?"

"He expressed some definite frustration with the team and with me on how we run meetings and how we decide things."

"That sounds like something we should discuss in more detail."

Max interrupted, "Yeah, especially after you hear what happened when I talked with my team earlier this morning."

"Yes, that was one of my questions, whether the team knew yet."

"Yep, they do."

"I was wondering if you considered the person who left to be your successor?"

"He was definitely the primary candidate."

"So that's playing into your surprise and frustration, I assume."

"For sure."

"Did he know that you considered him your successor?"

"No, we didn't talk about it . . . until yesterday."

"And that didn't make a difference to him?"

"Yeah, it did, but not enough of one. He did get a little sentimental about it, though."

"Sounds like he was a little bummed, too," I said.

Max did not acknowledge me, and in an instant, he changed his demeanor. "I've got to fill the gap as quickly as possible. Need to let the team know to get the word out that we're looking for someone, pronto."

"Hold on a second, Max. You are moving to 'fix-it' mode when you have not let yourself deal with the loss for more than two minutes. And besides, this may be a good time to step back and fill the position differently."

"What do you mean, fill the position differently?"

"Do you want to talk about this now?"

"Yeah, yeah. And I promise I won't run out and find the first person who might be able to do it."

"There's one principle I want you to consider first. Instead of filling a gap in your team, ask yourself: 'What great people are out there that I need to have on my team?' Hiring great people is the cornerstone of your success."

"OK, makes sense. And sounds kind of simple."

"It seems like it. Just hard to actually do, because normally we're pulled to quickly fill a gap. A couple of years ago, when I read Jim Collins's book *Good to Great*, I shifted my perspectives on how to hire people. The book addresses how great leaders get the right people on the bus, first, and then figure out where to go. It's such a simple concept, but think about it: In most corporations, the 'What' decisions come before the 'Who' decisions. We do vision, strategy, and a lot of organizational structure, including head-count analysis before we get the very best people."

"That's true. We do look at head-count needs and go from there, usually."

"In *Good to Great*, Jim Collins also says that when a manager has any doubt about a hire, he or she shouldn't hire and should keep looking."

"That's tough to do when we need to fill a spot in order to get things done quickly."

"It takes a lot of discipline not to fill it, and rigor to find the right person. Keep these concepts in mind as you are looking to replace the IT sales position. Go out and find a dynamo first. And then, you may have to shift some things around based on what he or she brings to the table. I'll help you to keep this front and center as you go through the hiring process, OK?"

"The first thing I need to do is put together a job description. This conversation has got me thinking in a different way. I probably want to be more big picture with the description, rather than narrow."

I nodded. Max paused for a couple of seconds, and at that point, I thought we should venture back to discussing the team meeting that he had held that morning.

"Let's go back to your team's reaction. You said you talked with them this morning?"

"Yeah, a can of worms got opened up in the meeting."

"What happened?"

"I told the team about the IT sales guy leaving. They were shocked, too. His role is integral to IT's success, and there are high stakes with the sales folks."

"Did they express their concerns to you?"

"Not exactly. I told them about the feedback I got, you know, about pocket vetos and disorganized meetings."

"Yes."

"They got really defensive about the pocket vetos, denied it, and then accused the guy leaving of doing it."

"Interesting."

"Then we talked about our meeting format. People have been frustrated about inconsistency—we cancel the meetings sometimes, and they never start on time, or end on time, for that matter."

"OK, were there other things people are concerned with?"

"Decision making. People were kind of pissed that I overrule some of what they think should be their decisions. They said that I do it without telling them and that they end up finding out way after the fact."

"Do they have a valid point? Do you do this?"

"I do, if I don't think things will fly with the VP of the group they support."

"What about the 'without telling them' until 'after the fact' part?"

"I don't think I do that, but a couple of them think I do."

"What are some ways you could manage your team's perception on how you make decisions?"

"I don't know, we have to make decisions quickly, and we can't round up everyone all the time."

"True. You can't round up everyone all the time. Your direct reports (and their direct reports) need to know when they can expect a consensus-type decision and when not to. Communicating how a decision is going to be made is as important as the decision itself."

"But sometimes there's not even time for that."

"I disagree. You have to make time to manage people's perceptions. Remember how upset you were when your boss jumped in on the 'project of projects'?"

"Yep."

"You were more upset that he changed the rules in the middle of the game—that he got involved and made decisions on the project when you weren't expecting it— than in the decisions themselves."

"So, you are saying that I should communicate how I'm making a decision and not worry about the decision itself?"

"No, they are both important, actually. I suggest that you manage people's expectations, and to do that you have to let them know how a decision is going to be made."

"OK, I can live with that."

"There's another tool that I would like to e-mail you that would be helpful with your team meetings. You had mentioned you received some feedback on meeting format, too, right?"

Max nodded.

"We can go over that next week, after you have had a chance to take a look at it. The tool is called the Communication Checklist. I think you will find it very useful. Also, Max, do you think it would be beneficial to you if I sit in on one of your staff meetings to get a sense of how you are running the meetings?"

"I don't know. Is that normal, to drop in like that?"

"Yes, I've been an observer in other VPs' team meetings. Your team already knows you are working with a leadership coach, right?"

"Yeah."

"Well, do you feel safe having me there?"

Max smiled. "I did up until this morning's meeting with the team. Just kidding." He paused. "I actually think it would be good for me and the team to get your input."

"Your regular staff meetings are on Thursdays; this morning was an emergency meeting, right?"

"Yeah, do you want to come this Thursday?"

"Let me check." I looked down at my PDA. "I can't meet this Thursday, but I could come next Thursday. Will that work?"

"Yeah, that will be fine."

"And that will also give us a chance to go over the Communication Checklist next Tuesday when we meet."

"OK."

"One last thing, Max, on a totally different subject: How are the networking meetings going? Has your assistant set up those meetings for you?"

"He has set them up, and I think I have my first meeting from that list late next week."

"Good. See you next week, Max."

— 10 —

Communication Checklist

I got an e-mail from Max late Monday night letting me know that his wife and son were really sick. He was planning on working from home on Tuesday, so we would need to cancel our meeting. He also said that he got the Communication Checklist from me via e-mail and would look it over, and that he was planning on presenting it to his team during their regular staff meeting on Thursday—the one I was going to observe.

Communication Checklist

Modalities	Primary Practices	Specific Actions
One-on-one meetings (phone or face-to-face)	✓ Update ✓ Brainstorm ✓ Feedback ✓ Decisions ✓ Requests	✓ Start and end on time ✓ Agenda and process goals agreed to at beginning of meeting ✓ Make conscious effort to establish rapport and track agenda ✓ Action items confirmed at end of meeting; make specific requests ✓ Regularly brainstorm/focus on strategic and innovative thinking
Group meetings	✓ Update ✓ Brainstorm ✓ Feedback ✓ Decisions ✓ Requests	✓ Set agenda with appropriate amount of time scoped to each agenda item ✓ Start and end on time ✓ Determine how meetings will be documented ✓ Have standing agenda items for weekly or biweekly team meetings ✓ Make conscious effort to track agenda ✓ Action items confirmed at end of meeting; make specific requests
Voice mails	✓ Update ✓ Feedback ✓ Requests	✓ Say your need/request in first 30 seconds ✓ No more than 2 minutes ✓ Summarize with 2 or 3 points
E-mails	✓ Update ✓ Feedback on written documents ✓ Requests	✓ Summarize updates before and/or after meetings ✓ Use to give status on initiatives ✓ Put "request for feedback, action, or information" and date needed in subject line
In-the-moment chats	✓ Update ✓ Feedback ✓ Decisions ✓ Requests	✓ Plan to include "walk-arounds" in your daily schedule ✓ Establish rapport quickly; ask "Is this a good time?" ✓ Be specific about what you need

11

Feedback

I greeted Max and asked how his wife and son were doing. He assured me that they were back at work and school, and everything was fine. Then I asked, "Max, what do you have on your list of topics for discussion today?"

He paused. "Just your impressions from last Thursday's team meeting."

"Let's do that, and I also want to touch base on the Communication Checklist. I'm curious what questions you have about it. In addition, I want to hear about the success of your VP networking meetings your assistant has been scheduling."

"OK."

I pulled out my notes from last Thursday's team meeting and began to recite my feedback in a way that was hopefully modeling an important skill. When I give feedback, I try to give as much evidence of behavior—

what I see and what I hear—rather than just a litany of interpretations.

"First, I noticed how your voice was clear and quick; this signified to me how upbeat and confident you seemed. You gestured with your hands and held people's attention."

"Did I use my hands too much or point? You know I've gotten that as negative feedback in the past."

"No, I think it was the right amount. I also liked how you asked good questions to get people to participate, and you did an excellent job of looking people in the eye when you addressed them. My interpretation of this is that people view you as sincere."

Max nodded, and I continued, "Your agenda was well organized and you stuck to it. Do you always have agendas?"

"No, I figured I would have one because I knew you were coming. We were definitely on our best behavior, so I don't know how realistic it was."

"This often happens, and my answer is the same every time: Being on your best behavior shows that you all can actually do it, with conscious thought. So now you should expect it more often," I said with a smile.

"Touché. So you are saying we have no excuse."

"Yes, that's exactly what I'm saying." I paused. "I do have suggestions for some improvements."

"Go for it."

"As I mentioned, you did get the group to participate, especially in the Communication Checklist conversation. Would you agree that the team has bought into trying to use the list?"

"Yes."

"They had some good additions about e-mail etiquette."

"Of all the things on that list, if we just got better at e-mail, I would deem that a success. Making clear requests on e-mail, and putting the 'date needed by' in the subject line is great."

I looked down at my notes. "I have some more feedback: When you were moving through the first part of the agenda on some of the business issues, you interrupted people quite a few times. I actually started counting, and it was eight times."

"It was that much?"

"Yes, in most instances, you did not let them finish their thoughts. A couple of times here or there is understandable in group meetings because people—including you—are competing for airtime; but eight times is a definite pattern that we need to address."

"Did I really do it that much? And do you really think it had a negative impact?"

I nodded my head more vigorously than normal. "It's a specific example of what your boss was talking about when we first started. He called it intensity, but did not give you any specific behavior to change. I've noticed that you do it with me sometimes, too; and I've chosen not to point it out to you. Now, though, I have more than my own experience."

"Wait a second. I think people expect that around here, that quick back and forth."

"I agree there's an expectation for a certain amount of it. If you cut the interruptions in half, my guess is that you would fall in line with the average person here."

Max was quiet for a couple of seconds. "It's that bad, huh?"

I looked at him with empathy and confidence. "It's definitely something you need to monitor; and if you don't monitor it, it could continue to lead to some people 'shutting down' or being afraid to voice their opinions in meetings. I did notice two people in your team meeting (out of the ten in the room) who did not participate at all, and two others who stopped contributing after they were both interrupted twice."

Max didn't say anything.

"You are not the only person doing the interrupting. But by you doing it, you are modeling it and unconsciously condoning it."

"Yeah, I get that I should stop. I mean, I don't like it when people interrupt me."

"Exactly."

"So, any more words of wisdom about how to curb my bad behavior—all the interrupting?"

I paused to determine whether he was being serious or sarcastic. "Sure, I have some thoughts. Are you game?"

He smiled. "It depends on what these thoughts of yours are."

"OK, on the interrupting, when you do catch yourself doing it, how do you know?"

Max stared at me for a moment. "I guess some of the time the other person just tells me to wait; I stop and let him or her finish. And sometimes, I guess the person has a certain look on his or her face that tells me I just might have bulldozed him or her."

"OK, that's good, you notice some *external* cue. One time during the team meeting I saw you catch yourself, and I happened to see the other person's face. That time, you did seem to use the person's facial expressions as a clue. So that's one way: Notice if the other person's body language changes. There are also some *internal* cues you can pay attention to as well."

"What do you mean internal cues?"

"When you get into that heightened sense of speedy back and forths, is there a place in your body that you can point to that feels different from other conversations?"

Max smiled. "You are definitely getting touchy-feely on me now."

I shot back, "You have a body, don't you?"

We both laughed out loud. I paused and thought that up until this point in our coaching sessions, we had not talked much about the relationship between emotions and the body. I realized I had an opening here, albeit one that stemmed from humor, and knew it was important to eventually ground the discussion in a rationale for better leadership. I said, "OK, Max, let's take an easier question: Where do you feel stress?"

"Definitely in my head. I get tense right here between my eyes."

"And what do you do with that biofeedback? For example, when you feel your head tense, do you do something different?"

"Yeah, it's usually a clue I'm not getting what I want."

"And do you then make an adjustment in the situation?"

"It depends. Sometimes I dig deeper, and sometimes I back off."

"You get feedback from your body, and you change your behavior, right?"

"OK, I get your point. So you want to know what my body is doing when I'm in the rapid back-and-forth, interrupting mode?"

I nodded. "Yes, for starters."

"Sometimes, I actually feel speedy inside, like a rushing feeling right here in my gut."

"When you feel that, do you make adjustments?"

Max paused longer than usual. "I'm not sure. I suppose the answer is 'No' because I don't think I get the body cue fast enough. I usually make an adjustment—like slowing down—when I see that the other person is getting angry or something."

"Are you willing to make an adjustment when you first feel this rush in your gut? It may curb a lot of your interruptions."

Max paused a long time. I didn't think he was convinced yet.

"Max, what's your resistance?"

Max leaned his head way back and sighed. "It's just a lot to think about, all these different skills and being so aware of my body."

"Does it seem too overwhelming?"

"Yeah, I don't know if I can do this and everything else."

"Are you having that tense feeling in between your eyes, right now?"

"Yeah, how did you know?"

"That's what you said earlier—what happens to you—when you get stressed."

"Oh yeah."

"And you're not feeling the rush in your gut—your stomach—right?"

"Right."

"What do you normally do to relieve the tension in between your eyes?"

"I usually get to walk to my next meeting, which means I get relief from the person who is causing the stress."

"Sorry, Max. I'm not going anywhere yet."

"I didn't mean you."

"I know. We have an opportunity to work on relieving that overwhelming feeling in the moment, right now. Do you want some relief?"

"Yes, definitely, because I have a huge meeting after this."

"OK, all I want you to do is take a conscious breath to your forehead. Breathe to where it's tense."

"This is kind of weird."

"Are you too uncomfortable?"

"No, no, it's cool."

"Max, my guess is that before a big presentation, you focus on your breath to calm your nerves, right?"

"Actually, yes."

"This is the same thing. You are just bringing your attention to your body through your breath in the *middle* of a stressful time, not just before it. Breathing itself centers you."

As I was talking, Max was taking deep breaths consciously. He started to smile. "Realistically, I don't think I'm going to be sitting in the middle of a meeting, then stop and take these big breaths."

"No, you don't need to be so demonstrative about it. You can stop for a moment, though, while someone else is talking, and breathe more deeply through your nose."

Max tried that, and got more comfortable. "I guess I never thought of focusing on my breathing in the middle of a meeting. Like you said, I usually do it to prepare for something." Max smiled. "This has been very helpful. Thank you."

"You're welcome." I took a conscious breath of my own. "One more thing: You know that speedy feeling you get in your stomach?"

"Yeah," Max responded.

"Breathing's good for that, too."

"So I suppose my practice for the week is 'just breathe.'"

"Yes, as long as you connect it to what you want: less stress and less interrupting, which, by the way, results in effective leading."

"Ah, we have come full circle, haven't we?"

"I try to make it all fit together." I looked down at my original goals for the meeting. "One more thing: I said I would check in on your VP networking meetings. Have you had any in the past two weeks?"

"Yep, I talked with the head of one of the business units. I asked him a number of questions about his strategic plan and his future IT needs."

"Sounds like it was a good meeting. How was the rapport with him?"

"It was easy. He goes faster than I do, so it was easy to pace him."

"Good." I started to get up to leave.

Max motioned me to stay. "One more thing: Any more feedback from the team meeting?"

I paused for a moment, and decided that Max was already overloaded. He had said it, and he looked it. "No, I've given you enough for now. Just focus on what we have talked about—breathe! See you next week."

— 12 —

Transition

Max greeted me with a big smile.

"You look really excited. What's up?" I asked.

"You were right about 'hiring the right people first.' The recruiter just called and said that since we opened up the search to a broader candidacy, we have received a lot more applicants, and some really talented people in other industries are coming through."

"Great."

"I know that this hiring process has taken longer than normal, but it's worth it if we can find someone who can bring in a breath of fresh air to IT, in general, and to the IT folks in the sales group particularly."

"Do you have a slate of candidates yet?" I asked.

"Yes, we do. We're bringing in four. One that stands out for me right now is this guy from a customer support team in Canada. He has been in a small consumer-products company, and wants to go back into a large corporation. I need to convince him to stay at a small corporation so he will have a bigger scope of work."

"What can he bring to the table that others may not?"

"The recruiter told me that he is really creative, quite the visionary about how service organizations work with business units. He has actually written some white papers and spoken at a couple of conferences about how to streamline the process."

"That sounds promising. Are there other candidates that intrigue you?"

"Yes, there are a couple of other guys from the IT world. One is a VP, who is interested because he wants to move here from New York because his family is out here. Another is a woman from a competitor who the recruiter is really high on."

"Does this new position require that he or she work with the sales organization like the former IT director did?" I asked.

"No, I definitely could move someone else over there. That's why I want to get the very best person I can."

"Max, I like the way you and the recruiter have shifted your focus on this one, and opened it up."

"Yeah, she has a good network of people. She is using her buddies in the search business to help identify some top folks. I've been very involved as well. I've asked her to keep me in the loop daily."

I realized that we had jumped right into what was on Max's mind—the new hiring. I had a number of things to talk about with Max, including checking in on goals and accomplishments, because we were at the three-month mark.

"What else did you have in mind to talk about today?" I asked.

Max shot back, "I don't want to talk." Then he slowed way down, enunciated every word with a wide smile, "I just want to practice breathing."

Without missing a beat, I asked, "Is that because you are used to it already, or because you have not been doing it?"

"Believe it or not, I've paid a lot of attention to it. One time, I even got distracted by my breathing and had to ask someone to repeat themselves, because I hadn't heard them the first time."

"I see the pendulum has swung to the other side. That's a good thing. Eventually, you will come back to the center, and it will feel more natural to focus on yourself and other people simultaneously."

"I have a confession." Max turned his eyes downward. "I know I've been kidding around a lot about this breathing stuff. You should know it has really helped. I feel less stressed than I did a week ago. I can't believe the difference it makes."

"That's great news."

"I'm curious about something. Do you ask all your clients to do the 'breathing thing'?"

"In some way or another, yes. It's rarely the first thing I start with. Even though it seems like such a simple practice, I introduce 'breathing' only when people are ready.

It's often hard for clients to understand how breathing relates to leadership."

"Yeah, I figured that. I gave you a hard time when you first told me. But I definitely get how being less stressed can result in more effective leadership."

"Exactly. I have a simple way of looking at this: Emotions and moods lead to *constructive* behavior, and can, just as easily, lead to *destructive* behavior. 'Being in touch' with your emotions—whether it's stress, sadness, excitement—is a key to being an effective leader."

"Keep going. I get the connection between emotions and leadership. How do you teach others about the 'breathing thing'?"

"Being in touch with your emotions requires that you be in touch with your body."

"Is there another way we can say that without using the 'being in touch' part? I want to be able to share this with others without sounding like we're going back to a 1960s' encounter group."

"What would sound better or look better to you?"

"How about 'If you want to know what your emotions are, you need to know what your body is doing'?"

"That's good and realistic. Because of its constancy, focusing on the breath is the best way to know your body. And if that's the only thing you focused on—consistently—you would be far ahead of most people, and most executives."

Max grinned, realizing that I was giving him a compliment for a job well done this week. He paused a moment and said, "I have one more question. Do you practice what you preach? Do you focus on your breath, like you have asked me to do?"

"Yes, I focus on my breath, especially to reduce distractions. I'm easily distracted."

"Really. I've never noticed."

"Good, because I work on it. I do a lot of conscious breathing. A lot more than I did five years ago, or even two years ago."

"So how did you learn or decide to do this?"

"You mean the breathing?"

"Yeah."

"I've learned it mostly through practice in meditation retreats. I decided to learn it because in my reading across disciplines—Buddhism, psychology, emotional intelligence, brain science, and somatics—the best way to understand the mind-emotion-body connection is through the breath."

"Interesting. You are not going to tell me I have to go to a meditation retreat, are you?"

"No, and you are not ready."

"Oh, thanks," Max responded sarcastically.

"No, I mean, when the time is right, we will talk about it. For now, being aware of your breath is a good goal, and you don't have to go to a retreat to know that. You just need to practice it in your everyday life."

"OK. Good discussion. Thank you." Max paused. "I want to change topics now; are you ready?"

I nodded and chuckled to myself, amused by Max transitioning us. I also noticed he thanked me, and that he had done this more often lately. A good sign that he was getting a lot of value and that he was slowing down.

"I want to tell you about my team meeting last Thursday. I really opened up the meeting for more feedback and brainstorming than usual. And I focused on not interrupting."

"Good. How did you do?"

"Fine. I made sure I was just facilitating and didn't say much. It's what happened after the meeting that I want to talk about."

"OK."

"One of my direct reports popped into my office a couple of hours later. She said that most of the team stayed for ten minutes after the meeting and nominated her to talk to me."

"What did she say?"

"She said that the team is excited about the new candidates and that they appreciate the opportunity to brainstorm more. And that the team definitely wants more of these kinds of meetings. They find them useful to get more clarity in terms of roles, direction, and objectives."

"It sounds like she had some requests in there."

"Yeah, she and I ended up talking for more than an hour. We concluded from the conversation that because we have someone new coming on board it's a good a time to look at formulating a new vision for the IT organization."

"And she thinks the team is up for that?"

"Yeah. And I think my boss would be in to it, too, given he wants me to focus on strategy more."

"You want to include the new IT director in the mix, right?"

"Definitely. It will be his or her first order of business."

"When are you hoping this person comes on board?"

"We're interviewing all this week and next. It's a short week next week because of Thanksgiving, so we will make an offer the first week in December. The person will probably want to wait to start until after the holiday break. I'll ask him or her to come in for a day to do the visioning thing with us. Hopefully, that will work out."

"It's cutting it close. And it's doable."

"Oh, by the way, I want you to help with the visioning thing."

I paused, nodded, and asked, "Are we going to call it 'the visioning thing'?"

"No. How about a 'new strategic direction'? My boss will like that."

"OK, how do you want me to help?"

"I want you to facilitate the day and help me put it together. You do that normally, right?"

"Yes, I often do this for the teams of the executives I coach."

"OK, good. Should we plan to spend some time on this next time we meet?"

"Yes, and I want to understand a bit more about your goals. How far-reaching, for example, do you want this vision to be? And do you have a team vision now?"

"We have a mission statement and we have organizational objectives based on the company strategy plan. We need something more inspirational and interesting. I want us to do Information Technology differently from other companies."

"Given what you want, I think it's important that you work on your personal vision first—this will set the tone for the organization. We have the time to do this, because we need to wait until you hire the new person."

"What do you want me to do?" Max asked.

"I have some questions; I call them 'personal legacy' questions. I'm taking next week off for vacation, so we are not meeting. Because you are going to be here interviewing candidates, you can work on these questions. Is that a deal?"

"Yeah, that will work."

"OK, good." I paused. "Max, I have one more thing. We are at the three-month mark in our work together, and I want to spend a couple of minutes surveying the goals we set at the beginning."

"No problem."

I pulled out the original agreement letter. "What do you see as your primary accomplishment in the area of 'better communications with team'?"

"The request-making skills have helped, for sure. Actions are clearer than they have been. I think people on the team are being more efficient. We still have to focus on the Communication Checklist," he stated firmly.

"Is there something specific on that list that you want to highlight in the next three months?"

Without hesitation, Max answered, "Yeah, definitely managing meetings better."

"OK, what about the goal 'being more strategic and influential with peers'?"

Max thought for a moment. "First, that skill you mentioned about being 'influenceable.' I like that because it turns influencing completely around. I influence through force sometimes." He lowered his eyes in a moment of reflection and continued, "Now I realize I don't want to be influenced that way, so I have to be more flexible when I'm trying to influence others."

"Good; how is it working?" I asked gently.

"Yet another skill I could work on the rest of my life, but I'm gaining ground," he said with a sparkle in his eyes. "Just yesterday, I backed off something with my peer in customer support. We were going back and forth for ten minutes, and I finally asked a question that got us unstuck."

"That's a good example. I remember when we talked about this you said you were a two or three on a scale of one to ten. Where are you now?"

"Probably a five and gaining."

"Good. What about 'being more strategic' with your peers?"

"I'm definitely in more conversations that I would consider strategic with my peers. And before I do too much more there, I want to focus strategically with my team, which we will be doing next month."

"OK, last one: How is your stress level?" I asked.

"I know I made fun of you when you asked me to focus on my breath and where in my body I was stressed. But doing that has really helped me." Max admitted.

"And what about the 'demanding' part?"

"I think I'm less demanding because I'm clearer, if that makes sense." he said.

I nodded.

Max continued. "I'm trying to get my requests and delegations clear the first time, so I don't have to go back so many times and be on people."

"Good. I have a request of you now. I'll e-mail you this list, and then I ask that you have a conversation with your boss about your goals and accomplishments thus far. Get his feedback as well. Will you get on his calendar before the end-of-the-year break?"

Max nodded and sarcastically replied, "Amidst everything, I'll do this."

"Good, I'll see you after Thanksgiving. Go easy on the turkey, Max!"

— 13 —

Building Blocks

During the Thanksgiving holiday week, I sent Max the set of questions that will serve as the building blocks of his *personal legacy*.

Values: What do you consider the five most important values that you live by?

Gift: What do you think your greatest gift (or skill) is as a leader?

Known for: When coworkers think of you, what are you most known for now?

Possible shifts: What do you want to be known for now that you are not yet known for?

Known for in the future: Imagine that I (your coach) was having a conversation with one of your friends 20 years from now. What would you want that person to say about you?

14

Personal Legacy

Max hustled in. "Sorry I'm late," he said, as he fumbled through his computer bag. "Let me get my notes. I spent time on those questions late last night."

I paused and noticed that his mind seemed to be racing. He confirmed my perceptions. "There's a lot going on today—especially, because we made the offer yesterday to the new guy. I also have a meeting with my boss later today I haven't prepared for yet."

"Let me guess: Did you go with the guy from Canada?"

"Yep, and he accepted, which we're thrilled about. We just need to hammer out the details, including immigration."

"Do you want to use some of our time today to prepare for your meeting with your boss?"

"Actually, we don't need to. I'll be OK; I actually want to focus on these legacy questions for the bulk of our session."

"OK."

Max started to read his responses slowly, with a little smile on his face. "First question—five most important values:

1. Hard work
2. Strive as high as you can
3. Integrity
4. Do more with less
5. Help whenever you can."

"These are great. What did you come up with for the second question?"

"My greatest gift as a leader—decisiveness."

"Did anything else come to mind?"

"Well, yeah, my drive and spirit. This, of course, is a double-edged sword. When we first started out more than three months ago, we talked about how my drive is good in order to get things done, but can be really negative because I can be hard on people."

"Yes, and that relates to number three."

"Yeah, what I am known for:

- Working hard (working too hard, actually)
- Setting high standards (too much of a driver, actually)
- Perseverance
- Problem solving
- Helping people see options

- Relentless
- Impetuous."

I chimed in, "Sounds like you added in the feedback you got from your boss when we first started."

"Yeah, I've been thinking this through more. I'm really ready to do something about my reputation. I get that perception is reality."

I smiled to myself, because I could hear the shift in his voice. His attitude was catching up to all the new behaviors he has been trying out. "You have already made some inroads, don't forget that."

Max stared back at his notes for a couple of moments; he looked up at me andk down at the notes. He took a deep breath, started to speak, and then stopped. I waited and wondered what he was feeling. Then he spoke, "You know, before I tell you what I want to be known for now that I'm not yet known for, I have to let you know that I'm mad at myself."

"What about?"

"Well, I know better. I shouldn't have to do this kind of exercise to be more compassionate," he divulged.

"Is that what you want to be known for, 'to be more compassionate' than you are now?"

"Yeah."

I deliberated whether to stay with the legacy questions or address his concerns. "Go easy on yourself, Max. These exercises are just reminders—reminders to be more conscious. Most people in the world value compassion;

the hard part is acting with it, especially because speed gets in the way of our ability to be compassionate."

"Definitely."

"We'll talk more about this. First, tell me, what's the last legacy question?"

"Twenty years from now, I would want one of my friends to tell you that 'Max is a wise guy.'"

He grinned, trying to make me laugh. It worked.

He continued, "My friends, as well as my colleagues, enjoy me because I'm a 'wise guy'—I joke around with them sometimes, and I'm quick and witty. But I don't want to go down in history as a 'wise guy who got things done.' Jeez! This has been gnawing at me all the way up and down the 101 freeway. What I really want them to say is he's 'a guy who is wise.'"

We sat quietly for a moment. More questions popped into my mind based on Max's responses: How would he describe a wise person? How would being wise help him and those around him? How would he remind himself to be more compassionate?

"A guy-who-is-wise," I repeated slowly. "You want to be wise; wiser than you are now?"

"I really don't consider myself wise. I think I'm clever. Being wise and being clever are different."

"Great distinction; tell me more about the difference."

"I use my experience a lot like a wise person, but I get into things and out of things because I'm clever. Every day, people come to me with issues that have to be solved. I get into the problem by understanding the angles; I get out of the problem by coming up with a few clever ideas and letting the person know what I think. It's quick and transactional so I can go to the next problem."

"OK."

He continued, "I guess I don't view a wise person as looking at the world through a series of problems."

"Instead, you see a wise person as . . . ?" I asked.

"I see a wise person being patient and empathetic."

"Do you want to be more of these things?"

"Yes, *and* I want to be clever."

"I like that, and I agree with you!" I paused and thought this would be a good time to delve a little deeper. "So, Max, what else do you think distinguishes wisdom?"

"Having vision, which is yet another reason why I want to spend time on this personally and with the team."

"How do you know someone is visionary?"

"They look toward long-term possibilities and aren't always caught up in the latest crisis."

"Hard for us driver types to do, right?"

Max nodded. "There are very few visionaries around here. There are strategists but not necessarily visionaries."

"How do you see the difference?"

"Strategy doesn't seem as innovative as vision."

"Say more."

"We're always talking about aligning strategy to the corporation; vision seems to be outside the box or, literally, outside the line," Max explained.

"I would agree with that. Another distinction is strategic planning and strategic thinking. Planning is something most companies do once a year; strategic thinking is a skill that could and should be used every day. Most strategic thinkers are visionaries."

"Yeah, that's good. I want to do more strategic thinking every day."

"Being a visionary definitely takes time. There's something else that's tricky about it. A visionary is usually thought of as someone who can see the future clearly, without controlling it. A visionary is able to see the future and stays present without being too attached to the future."

Max interjected, "Pretty impossible in this results-oriented culture."

I paused for a moment. Should I merely agree and move on here? I wanted to be empathetic; yet, I think Max needs to be stretched here. Results orientation is one of the characteristics that defines Max—it's what he is known for and what he is good at. I could support him best by stretching him in a different way—to think about being able to reflect amid the chaos. I went back to a metaphor we had talked about a couple of months ago.

"I disagree, Max. I see people who actually get better results at different speeds. Think about gear shifts—remember we talked about that awhile back. Sometimes we need to be in fifth gear, most of the time we're in third or fourth. And sometimes we need to stop and be still, you know, idle a bit," I smiled.

"Yeah, I remember you talking about it. I don't think it's sunk in yet, though."

"To think about the future and to be present—in either case—stillness is required. Thinking about future possibilities requires quiet time at some point in your day. And presence requires a stillness of mind in the moment."

"I can accept going slower—like being in first gear. But stillness, that's stretching it." Max said, "Come on, now, how are you able to do that?"

I paused and took a conscious breath. "Well, I'm doing it now. I'm focusing on my breath. I'm giving myself a tiny moment to gather my thoughts and to express what is most true for me. At the same time, my attention is on you and what is best for you in this moment."

"Oh yeah, the breath," he grinned.

"I use the breath to slow me down. Some say a word to themselves; others have a sticky note in front of them to remind them."

I took another conscious breath and waited for Max to respond.

"Hmm. I think I still need a big billboard to remind me to breathe," he declared.

I started to say something to match his humor and then stopped myself. I took another conscious breath. "I say all of this because of the theme that keeps popping up here: You want to be more compassionate. I thought you may want to know what I associate compassionate with."

Max started to interrupt, stopped himself, and waited until I was finished. "I get it—you associate being still with being compassionate."

I continued to offer a way for Max to find the compassionate part of him: "There's both a wise part of you and a decisive problem solver part of you. There's an impatient, task-oriented part of you and a patient, compassionate part of you. Thus far in your career, the decisive, task-oriented parts of you have served you best. You know this and it keeps reinforcing itself. Your compassionate side is there; you just need to practice."

"Old habits die hard."

"I realize this. That's why attitude helps. What's motivating you to work on the compassionate, wise part of you?" I asked.

"Well, two reasons: First, as you know, my results-orientation, hard-driving style is just too intense for people."

"Yes, I understand."

Max continued, "That question about what a friend would say about me in 20 years really got to me. I don't want people to think I'm slick and witty. I want to be known for helping others. So far in my life I've helped others by giving money. That's not good enough. I do need to give quality time. I'm just worried it's going to be too hard for me to slow down. I really do need that big billboard flashing before me."

I smiled. "Besides the billboard, what are you going to do to remind yourself to slow down?"

"Well, I like the idea of a sticky note, but because I can't exactly put a sticky note on my Palm Pilot, I could program a word to pop up every time my Palm Pilot reminds me of a new meeting."

"Creative. I like it—high-tech compassion. What word would be motivational for you?" I asked.

"*Compassion* seems too long." Max paused for a second. "*Care* would work. I can put a sticky note on my folder that I carry to meetings."

"And once you are in these slower moments, how will you know that you are acting with compassion, with care?"

"Well, we've talked about this before—I won't be interrupting as much. I'll pause more so I can really take in what the other person is saying. Compassion is about understanding so I need to understand more of what's going on."

I smiled to myself because in that moment, I felt Max really got it. In our three and a half months of working together, he had agreed to and started to change his behavior—to slow down, not interrupt as much, and ask more questions. Right now, I sensed that his deeper values now aligned with his behavior. He wasn't acting differently just because his boss wanted him to.

"You are beginning to define more of who you want to be—more of your personal legacy. You know, Max, you don't have to wait until you're 60 years old to be considered a corporate sage."

Max recited it slowly, "'Corporate sage.' That's interesting. I like the idea of being more of a sage."

"I thought it might resonate with you."

"If it helps me feel less overwhelmed and be a much more effective leader, then yes it definitely resonates with me." Max continued, "Thanks for all your help with these questions. This exercise has been good for me. I would like my team to work with these questions, too."

"Great, that's one of the exercises I had in mind when we get together in a couple of weeks."

"By the way, I did tell the new guy we would like him here for a day on December 15. He was cool with it."

"Good. Let's spend next week preparing for that day, OK?"

"Got it."

—— 15 ——

Team Legacy

Max was on the phone, but he motioned for me to come into his office anyway. It took him about five minutes to finish up the call, so I got a chance to listen to his end of the phone call. It turns out it was one of his peers, the VP of sales; Max was talking with him about the new hire, the senior director of IT.

Max slammed down the phone, twirled around in his chair, and said, "You convinced me it was important to get the very best person available, even though it was outside our industry; now I have to convince the VP of sales."

"He's not happy with your choice?"

"He did interview our top two, and he liked the other one better. But the team and I are sure we hired the right person. My boss liked him, too."

"Are you still planning on having the new hire act as the liaison to the sales VP?"

"I did talk with him about it. I could have the new guy work with marketing, including the Web folks, and have someone else work with sales. The new guy has an interesting background. In his most recent job, he was a head of customer support in a consumer-goods company. Before that, he ran IT for a small company that develops sales/contact management software. Given his background, I thought he would be perfect for the sales group."

"What does the VP of sales have a problem with?"

"He is more of a traditionalist; he wanted a guy, and I really mean 'guy,' who has done the exact job before."

"So did you come to any conclusions on the phone?"

"Yeah, I'm going to have one of my other IT people go talk with him, to see if they click. If that works, then the new guy will go into the marketing/Web slot."

"What does the new person think of this? Did you promise him the sales slot?"

"No, he was cool with either one. In anticipation of this, I did have him interview with the marketing head, who, by the way, is thrilled with him."

"That's good," I said.

"Enough about this. It's pretty much under control. I want to talk about the team and the visioning work we're going to do next week."

"That's my plan, too. Before we start with that, though, I want to check in about a few things."

"OK."

"How has your stress level been in the past couple of weeks?"

"It's manageable, I would say."

"Are you paying more attention to your body cues?" I pointed to my forehead, where Max had said he feels most of his stress.

"I am, actually. Most of the time I notice it when I'm at my desk by myself or after a meeting, not so much when I'm in the middle of something."

"Good, that's a start. It sounds like you are more aware of it now than in weeks past."

"Definitely."

I took a deep conscious breath. "And once you notice the tension, are you using your breath to relieve it?"

"Yes, I am. Not all the time, but some of the time."

"Realize, Max, this is going to take months to change. Remember, little by little."

"I am trying to be patient."

"What about the speedy feeling in your stomach? I'm curious, did you notice it when you were on the phone earlier with the sales VP?"

"I noticed I interrupted him a couple of times."

"Did you make any adjustments once you realized it?"

"It was hard, because I was kind of pissed."

"Yes, this is an example of those destructive emotions."

"I noticed that your voice tempo changed from when I first came into your office and when you finished the call. You were slower and had a softer tempo at the end. Did you make that adjustment consciously?"

"No, not exactly. I did slow down when I realized I had interrupted him. I wasn't aware of slowing down at the end of the conversation."

"The good news is that you did slow down; now, you need to become more conscious of it, so you can be more consistent. There is skill in the awareness, and there is skill in the adjusting."

"OK."

"This holds true for all the leadership skills we have talked about—request making, rapport, inquiry and advocacy, influencing—you have to become aware first before you can adjust. Another way to look at it: Get on the 'observation deck' for a moment, so you know what to change in-the-moment."

"The observation deck—I kind of like that."

"Perhaps it's a metaphor that you can remember easily, especially in the heat of an important meeting."

"I'll remember that. So, let's talk about the team."

"You said last week that you want the team to do some work on their personal legacy like you did, right?"

"Yep."

"Tell me, any afterthoughts to that discussion we had last week on compassion?"

"I did talk with my wife about the legacy questions and my responses a couple of nights after you and I had talked. We got a baby-sitter and went out for dinner on Friday night."

"And . . . ?"

"She was stunned and thrilled at the same time. She really is the compassionate one in the family. She was great about listening. She was very supportive."

"That's great."

"I also asked her to help me. I told her I want to spend more time at home with her and my little boy. I told her I would stick to the schedule, that I'd be better about coming home when she's expecting me. We talked about how I can get more involved with my kid's school. She suggested that we coach one of his teams together. He's really into soccer and basketball."

"Wow, sounds like it was one of those transformative kinds of conversations."

"Yeah, it was for me. I can't expect that this personal legacy process will be as valuable for everyone on my team, but at least I want to offer them the opportunity." Max reverted to his task orientation: "So what should we do with them; do you want me to e-mail them the legacy questions?"

"Yes, it would be a good idea that they come from you. Will the team come prepared by responding to the legacy questions before they come to the team retreat?"

"Yes, I'll request it of them. They'll do it."

"Good, be sure in the e-mail to let them know they'll be sharing their responses with their teammates and you."

"OK. I guess that may make a difference in their responses."

"It might. It's important to set their expectations." I paused for a moment. "Let me put on my consultant hat and talk a little about what I envision for the retreat."

"Go for it."

"In the first part of the retreat, the group will spend about half an hour in pairs discussing their responses to the legacy questions."

"That makes sense."

"Next, I'll ask each person to come up with one word that he or she wants to be known for, like when you came up with the word *care*."

"OK."

"Then, we'll get into a discussion on team legacy. I think the best way to do this, to encourage out-of-the-box thinking, is to use some questions as the basis for the discussion."

I showed him the *five-for-the-future* list and gave him a chance to soak it in.

Five years from now, what do you see the world being like (consider economy, politics, health, society, etc.)?

Five years from now, how will technology affect global business?

Five years from now, how will Solano contribute to global business?

Five years from now, how will Solano IT influence the IT industry?

Five years from now, how will IT influence Solano, overall, as a business?

Max smiled and said, "This is interesting. You're asking us to think really big at first and definitely out-of-the-box."

"Yes, there are two goals here. First there's the take-away: a vision statement that people are excited about. Think of it as an internal marketing tool because it's a vision that signifies what you, as a team, want to be known for. It's a stretch goal, something you're not known for now, and something you can all rally around."

"That makes sense."

"In order to get to that compelling take-away, instead of aligning ourselves with what already is, we want to create a vision based on our best guesses for the future. I want us to think of the IT industry in a context of business, society, and globalization. These questions—while at first may seem way out there—will get all of us thinking on a much grander scale."

"Yeah, I was wondering about that, five years seems awfully far away."

"We'll reel it in when we actually formulate the vision." I showed him the *shared vision* questions we could use.

What is the team's current mission?

What is your group known for now?

What do you want your group to be known for in two years?

What is a clear *and* compelling two-year vision?

What high-level strategies need to be in place to get you there?

Max nodded his head as he was reading. "Will we discuss these shared vision questions all together or individually, or what?"

"We'll do the five-for-the-future questions together as a large group, then the shared vision questions in three small groups first before we report to the whole team. At that point, we'll synthesize what each of the groups has done to make one vision. It's a lot to do, but we should be able to get to everything in one day."

"Should I send the team the organizational legacy questions in advance as well?"

"Probably not. Too much rumination beforehand may kill creativity in-the-moment. Let's have the team just do the personal legacy questions for homework."

Max asked, "I assume that I get to be a participant in this, and that I don't have to facilitate?"

"Yes, with one caveat. Will you begin the day with some appreciative words for them to remind them that they came to you with the idea to do more visioning? You may also want to mention that in your e-mail. It's vital that they get ownership in this."

"Got it."

"I'll see you bright and early next Wednesday with the team." I looked at my PDA quickly. "We skip two weeks through the holidays, and then, you and I meet one-on-one the first week in January."

— 16 —

Shared Vision

"Happy New Year, Max." I handed him a bottle of wine. "Here is a little holiday gift for you."

He read the card out loud. "Here's to you, on your way to becoming a corporate sage."

"Thanks very much, that's very thoughtful," Max said after he pondered for a few seconds. "You know, I do feel like I can, indeed, be more sage-like. The holiday break did me some good. I'm well rested."

"That's great. You stayed home for the past ten days and vegged?"

"For the most part. Except I did fly down to LA for the Rose Bowl game."

"Oh, yes, your home team—Ohio State—played. You must be bummed that USC squeaked by with the win."

"Yeah, but it was a great game, down to the wire. And we kicked their 'you-know-what' two years ago in the National Championship game."

"Yes, I saw that game. It was a sad day in my family's household."

"Wait a second, I thought you were a big Stanford fan?"

"I am, but my dad and aunt went to USC, so I root for the Trojans . . ." I paused and smiled broadly.

Max interjected, "Let me guess, except for when they play Stanford, right?"

"You got it."

I thought to myself: Given our propensity for sports, Max and I could spend our entire session on it. Instead, I guided us to our work at hand. "Max, I know we said we would go over the data from the retreat. Is there anything else that's on the top of your mind?"

"Yeah, the 49ers, they're in their first playoff game this weekend. Are you going?"

I chuckled to myself: I guess Max is not ready to hang up the sports conversation just yet. "Yeah, I'm working my network for tickets. How about you?"

"Naw, I'm going to have a few friends over and watch it at home," he said.

I smiled. "So any other teams you want to talk about?"

"Naw, let's get to work. Let's talk about the retreat. There's nothing else on my mind because I just got back the day before yesterday, and not too many people are around, really."

"We didn't get much of a chance to debrief right after the retreat. First, what was your overall impression of how the team worked together?"

"That it was the best I've seen the team get along in months. People spouted off and interrupted each other some of the time, but not as much as usual. I think doing the personal legacy work first helped. It was interesting and gave people a chance to get to know each other better. It also seemed to put people in a good mood."

"I agree."

Max continued, "And I'm really impressed with our new IT director. He had some awesome ideas. I think we landed a star."

"I'm impressed with you for having the guts to hire him. He is a real go-getter; he's got the drive and the creativity to do a great job."

"Well, he definitely has the potential to move up in the organization fast, and possibly be my successor. But I'm concerned he may be alienated by some of my other direct reports."

"What do you think is behind that?"

"People get jealous or envious of stars sometimes."

I paused for a moment, and wondered if Max was projecting—that *he* may be jealous of the new guy. I did not believe this to be the case, but I wanted to be sure before we moved on. "Max, I'm wondering: Are you, in any way, jealous of him?"

Max shot back quickly, "No, I'm psyched to have someone of his caliber here. I assure you I'm not jealous nor even envious; I'm relieved, actually. I need this guy here now more than ever."

"OK, I get that. I just wanted to be sure."

"One of the things my first boss told me was 'Hire people who are smarter than you are.' That has stuck with me ever since—that was 20 years ago."

"Definitely good advice. I am curious: What leads you to believe that your direct reports may be jealous or have alienated the new guy?"

"I was watching people a lot during the retreat. The new guy got cut off more than a couple of times, and I'm happy to report, I wasn't one of the people doing it."

"Yes, I noticed that, too. And I'm not so sure I would attribute that to jealousy."

"No, no, it's not just that. I had a couple one-on-ones with people before the holiday break, and several people told me they thought that you and I let him have the floor too much."

"Interesting. Any more evidence?"

"It's just a sense I have."

"Is there something you can pinpoint that will give him a heads up? He hasn't even officially started yet, right?"

"No, he starts next week. I can give him some feed-back when he comes in."

"What will you tell him?" I asked.

"I want him to get to know everyone one-on-one. Maybe I'll suggest he do interviews like you made me do."

"That I 'made' you do?"

Max smiled, "Well, you know, highly suggested that I do."

"Sorry to be the word police there, Max, but I hope I'm not 'making' you do anything."

"I'll ask him to do those interviews, both with the team and with his clients, right away."

"Good idea. Anything else you noticed at the retreat?"

"We're horrible at brainstorming. We have to get better at understanding why the other person thinks the way they do, instead of just assuming. During the first exercise, the *five-for-the-future* one, you had to ask us three different times to not comment on or criticize other people's ideas. It's like we automatically see the gap in someone else's argument or idea."

"Yes, these are habits that are hard to break. I do believe the group got better at this as the day went on."

"Really?"

"Yes, because people did some conscious course correction. You are not going to have me there at every meeting, though, pointing it out."

"That's for sure."

"You could ask for a volunteer each meeting—whether it's for one hour or all day—to be the 'process person.' This person would hold the team accountable to the Communication Checklist—whether it's brainstorming, decision making, getting updates, etc."

"Does that really work?"

"Yes, I've seen it work for other teams. It's something to think about." I paused to determine where to focus the rest of our time together. "Are you ready to talk about the vision?"

"Yes, go for it."

"I took the one we formulated together and made a few tweaks, really just wordsmithed it, and put it all in the present tense. I think it's important to write a vision in the present tense even though it's a future endeavor. It gives people more of a sense of possibility." I paused. "You got my edits, right?"

"Yeah, let me get it. I printed it out yesterday."

"Read it aloud, Max. Let's hear how it sounds."

"OK, here goes: Solano IT creates unprecedented value for our worldwide internal clients by providing comprehensive and easy-to-use solutions that result in giving Solano a competitive advantage and establishes IT as core to the business."

"Max, it rolls off your tongue pretty well. What do you think?"

"Like you said at the retreat, it needs to be clear, compelling, and useful. I think it's all those things. That 'future' exercise really stretched us to think more globally, beyond our little cubicles. It's short and pretty easy to remember. I hope we use it."

"What do you want to do next?" I asked.

"We need to develop some strategies. And I think we should realign our present initiatives. At the end of the retreat, we started talking about things like the importance of developing internal and external partnerships, and acquiring the skills to anticipate changing business needs. We need to add these to our initiatives."

"When will you continue the conversation with your direct reports?"

"It's already on the calendar for next week on Wednesday. I want to crank out the strategies in a couple of hours."

"It may take you a couple of meetings. Definitely by the end of the month, you will have the vision roadmap—the vision, strategies, and realigned initiatives. I think you will do a good job of facilitating the group, given what we have talked about today. Your awareness of group dynamics is improving rapidly."

"Thanks."

It was important to discuss the integration of the vision roadmap into the organization. "Max, remember when you went to Boston, and the GM was adamant that you and your team address the change-management issues?"

"Yeah."

"Same holds true with this integration. How are you going to ensure that people in your organization share in the vision, and use it to inform what they do every day?"

"Wow, that's a big question."

"Visions work well only if they are shared. This does not mean that everyone has to design it together. It's good that you and your management team have formulated a clear direction; employees like that. What is important, though, is that the vision has meaning for everyone every day. Each person has to make it their own in some small way."

"Well, first we have to communicate the vision roadmap. We can get it laminated; we can put it on our internal Web site . . . I'll present it to the whole organization, and each of my directs will discuss it with their teams."

"That's a good start."

Max paused, then stretched back in his chair. "Uh-oh, I'm getting the picture that there's much more to it than that."

I nodded, which confirmed his fears.

"What, then, do you suggest?"

"Wait a second, Max, I'm not going to just give you the answer. Think about it; put yourself in your employees' shoes for a minute. What compels *you* to buy in to something and embrace it?"

"A person being passionate helps. But not too passionate because I don't want something rammed down my throat."

"True."

"Sometimes when I hear a really inspirational speaker —and it takes a lot to inspire me—I like to figure out how I'm going to put that person's idea or vision into action. I ask myself, 'How can I go use this tomorrow?'"

"That's fantastic. That's your lead-in."

"My lead-in?"

"Your lead-in to your 'presentation' introducing the vision to your organization. Notice I'm putting presentation in quotes. Make it a very short presentation, and then spend most of your time facilitating a 'vision-into-action' discussion."

"Translate please; what do you mean?" Max asked.

"Remember when we were talking about your personal legacy, and we talked about being a visionary?"

"Yeah."

"Your initial passion is a cornerstone of being a visionary. Others may get fired up to do something different immediately," I said.

"What about the long-term effects; isn't that what being a visionary is all about?"

"Yes, that's another cornerstone. A vision becomes reality only if it's sustained over time. That happens because of the actions created over and over again. And the best way I know how to sustain actions over time is . . ."

Max interrupted, "Coaching."

I smiled broadly. "I don't mind the interruption. I think you realize now why having a couple of PowerPoint presentations and handing out a few laminated cards isn't going to sustain what you want. Your passion may give others the 'immediacy' needed to jump-start the change. Your coaching will help 'sustain' the change. Here you have the beginnings of your organization's legacy."

Max paused, leaned way back in his chair again, and said, "I'm starting to get that feeling in between my eyes."

"Oh yes, that overwhelming-stress feeling. Are you wondering how you can do this on top of everything else?"

Max nodded vigorously.

"If I told you that coaching to your vision doesn't take any extra time, would you be interested in learning the finer points?"

"OK, you got me interested."

"We'll work on coaching next week."

COACH IN-THE-MOMENT TO BUILD A LEGACY

Leader as Coach

Moment-to-Moment

Max walked in a couple minutes late and apologized. He greeted me and asked, "So you promised me that we would talk about coaching, right?"

"Yes. I did."

"Good, I want some pointers because I just spent an hour with one of my direct reports solving a bunch of her team's problems."

"Did *you* solve them or did *she* solve them?"

Max paused and smiled. "Little of both, I guess."

I smiled back, and was about to ask him to rewind the internal movie tape, when Max interrupted my thoughts.

He said, "Well, I think it was actually more of me telling her what to do; she was not getting anywhere, and going round and round. I actually didn't realize all that she has been up against. She needed to be reeled in a bit."

I thought it was a good time to bring up one of his past promises to himself. "Max, early last month, when we were talking about your personal legacy, you mentioned you wanted to demonstrate more compassion. Where were you on the compassion barometer with her?"

"Medium to low, probably."

"And what would make it medium to high?"

"Same old, same old. Got to slow down and ask more questions."

"There's something else, too. Your being good at problem solving serves you well in the operations side of your job. It's not going to cut it when you are coaching."

Max nodded. "Yeah, it's the old saying, right? Give someone a fish, and they have food for a day; teach someone to fish, and they have food for a lifetime."

I grinned. "Teaching someone to fish is one of the most sage-like things you can do. How often would you say, Max, you are teaching people to fish during a given week?"

"Not that much; I am solving problems most of the time, and moving to the next issue."

"So would you say 5 percent of the time right now?"

"No, I wouldn't even say that much."

"OK, let's say this: Of the time you spend with your direct reports, how much of that do you want to have 'teach-to-fish' conversations?"

"Definitely more than I do now; let's say a third of the time."

"Good, so you agree you want to teach to fish more. What do you need to do differently in order to coach more?"

Max shot back quickly with a grin on this face. "Ask a lot more questions, sort of like what you are doing now."

Max seemed to like that he was on to me. I was probably overplaying the Socratic method. Yet I wanted to demonstrate that, once again, good questions work.

I responded, "Right. Sometimes, managers and executives don't like to bother with a series of questions because they think giving the answer takes less time. And it does in the short term. But the long-term effects are discussions on the same subjects over and over. I like to hear leaders ask 'What are your options?' as the standard response when a direct report is looking for the answer."

"Yeah, I do that sometimes, when I'm not in a hurry."

"The good news with you, Max, is that you believe coaching is important, and that you want to focus on it. As a general rule, when executives are coaching, they are doing it formally in one-on-ones for performance reviews or problem solving."

"Yep."

"I think you can coach informally as well, using the bits of time in between meetings, on the phone, or even in the parking lot to give feedback and help our direct reports deal with issues or solve problems quickly."

"The parking lot—are you kidding?"

"The parking lot, the elevator, walking people to their next meeting, and stopping by your direct reports' cubicles or offices. The key is to leverage the time you do have, to coach 'anytime, anywhere.'"

Max stared at me in disbelief.

"Remember the end of our conversation last week: I promised you that coaching to the team's vision would not take any extra time."

"Yeah, I did not believe you then and I'm not sure I believe you now."

"I don't think coaching has to take any extra time, as long as you leverage the time you do have, whether it's informal drop-bys or formally scheduled meetings with your direct reports. Did you ever read *The One Minute Manager* by Ken Blanchard?"

"Yeah, a long time ago."

"He advised managers to walk around a lot, to get out of your office. It's more than that, because now given how virtual our work world is getting, we have to do 'call-arounds,' too, not just 'walk-arounds.'"

Max thought for a moment, and asked, "Do you do this coaching 'anytime, anywhere'?"

I nodded. "With my company's staff, I do a lot of coaching in between client meetings on the cell phone in my car. Because the company is mostly virtual, a lot of my in-the-moment coaching is on the phone. Regarding clients, as you know, all my clients are welcome to call me anytime to do a quick ten-minute in-the-moment coaching session on the phone in between your regular weekly sessions."

"It's such a great concept, to coach on-the-fly or, as you say, in-the-moment. Yet, I know I don't take advantage of the time in between meetings at all. I do like the idea of walking to the next meeting and solving a problem along the way. Actually, I do that now because people grab me after a meeting to get my approval on a lot of things." He paused. "But I wouldn't call approving things coaching."

"No, it's operational management." I hesitated a moment and then said, "I'm wondering how many of those 'approval' times could be turned into in-the-moment coaching opportunities."

"I will pay more attention to this."

I didn't push Max for specifics and decided to guide the conversation to the content of coaching. "When you do coach, what are the issues you tend to talk about? Be as specific as you can."

"Well, the obvious ones are problems that come up with my direct reports' internal clients or issues that my direct reports have with their direct reports, like today."

"Good. What about the vision you just created with your team? What kinds of questions could you ask about the vision in-the-moment as you are walking around?"

"Well, the whole point of the vision, like we discussed last week, has to do with putting it into practice. So I would ask about that. Something like, 'How have you put the vision roadmap into practice?'" Max pondered the question more. "Or I could just ask, 'What are you working on?' and go from there."

"Excellent. The hard part is taking the time to walk around and ask."

"It definitely makes a lot of sense in between meetings, on my way from one to the next."

"Not only is coaching important in terms of feedback on performance and problem solving, it's also vital to sustain a cultural shift like a vision. New visions take months to instill into the culture. It doesn't happen overnight, but through many coaching conversations—short ones and long ones."

"I need to tell my directs to ask questions and coach their direct reports in order for this vision to take hold, right?"

"You could give them an edict or you could talk with them—like I'm talking with you now—about leveraging in-the-moment coaching opportunities 'anytime, anywhere.' Coaching is good for a lot of things: building vision and legacy, performance feedback, and solving problems."

Now that Max had demonstrated that he understands some of the uses of coaching, I wanted to spend time with him on the process of coaching. "Would you like some pointers on *how* to coach effectively? These practices will help you coach well during your formal one-on-ones as well as during your walk-arounds."

"Go for it."

"As we have talked about, the core of any coaching is the ability to ask relevant, timely questions, but there's more to it than that. In-the-Moment Coaching—or **ITM** Coaching, for short—leverages coaching moment-to-moment." I showed Max the three-step method. "It's simple to remember: *rapport, assess, reframe.* It spells RAR."

ITM Coaching Model

Rapport: Clear distractions and build rapport quickly by matching body language, voice tone, and tempo.

Assess: Clarify the situation to understand the issue and help "set" the problem.

Reframe: Reframe words, thoughts, and actions to help others solve the problem.

I continued, "We have talked a lot about rapport already, when you were preparing for your peer interviews, remember?"

"Yes, and I think I am doing it regularly. I am especially focusing on what I want to get better at—matching tempo. I'm being more aware of slowing down to match the person I'm with."

I smiled. "Great job, Max. Building rapport is especially imperative in coaching. It's not just about matching behavior—in your case, slowing down—it's also about clearing distractions. Perhaps more than any other time in your day, when you are coaching, you have to be focused and totally present with the other person."

"So once again, you are asking me to slow down."

"You got it—slow down so you can demonstrate a special concentration. You want the other person to be the only person that matters to you in that moment."

"Makes sense. What about the assess part of the model? Isn't that like inquiry, like we talked about before?" Max asked.

"Yes and no. The skill of assess in coaching is not just about asking questions to clarify what the other person's situation is. It's those things and more. When you assess, it's also important to *set* the problem so you can help your direct report get unstuck and eventually *solve* the problem."

"What do you mean set the problem?"

"Take the situation you started with this afternoon: You said one of your direct reports needed to be 'reeled in.'"

"Yeah, definitely, she had three different things going on. One of her engineers has a performance issue, another wants to be promoted, and another has quit."

"So you have some choices about which issue to work on with her. Setting the problem is like priority setting. Your job as a coach is to listen, let the person vent for a while, and then help the individual decide which path to go down. Which one is the most important right then? Which one can be solved with your help?" I paused to let Max take this in.

"I'm thinking about another conversation that I had late last week. Setting the problem would have come in handy. One of my direct reports was really upset during our regular one-on-one. He spent the first ten minutes venting about a variety of issues."

"What could you do next time in order to set one of those problems before you and he start to solve it?"

"I should ask him, 'Which issue do you want to address now?'"

"Good; it's direct. Before you ask that question, you may want to summarize what you are hearing, like, 'You have mentioned these three things,' and then name them.

And then ask what you said, 'Which issue do you want to address now?'"

"That's a good one."

"Will you try this out next week?" I asked.

"Yeah, I will. If it comes up."

I wanted to be sure there were no hindrances to Max practicing the skill. "Are you sure you want to take this on?"

"I'm just not sure how much opportunity there will be."

"Look for the opportunity in places you don't expect. Walk one of your direct reports to his or her next meeting instead of jumping on your PDA."

"OK." Max looked down at his notes. "What about the reframe part of ITM Coaching? We didn't talk about that yet."

"Let's talk about that next week. For now, I want you to focus on the assess aspect of coaching: (1) asking good questions to understand the situation, and (2) setting the problem. We will look at ways to reframe when we get together next time."

Max deadpanned, "So, you don't want me to solve problems this week?"

I tried not to laugh, because I needed to give him an important suggestion: "No, I want you to focus on asking good questions and see if the people you are engaging solve the problem themselves."

"OK, I'll see how that works. See you next week."

— 18 —

Gems

Max greeted me with a huge smile, like he was up to something. "I have something fun to tell you about," he revealed. "I did a little experiment this past week."

"Really, what?"

"I started counting how many times in the day somebody came to me for an approval either by phone, in person, or through e-mail. And I counted how many times I was in an informal or formal meeting to problem solve."

"What did you find out?"

Max looked down at the scribbles in his notebook. "Get this: I averaged four official approvals per day, mostly through e-mail. People came to me for in-person approval when they had deadlines and I had not yet responded to their e-mail requests."

"Does this information surprise you?"

"A little I think. I thought I was doing a better job delegating. Some of the approvals are purchase orders that I've had to sign off on."

I nodded, and Max continued, "But some are project go-aheads."

"And those are the opportunities when you can teach your direct reports to fish, right?"

"Definitely. And there's another statistic I can do something about: I was in an average of eight meetings a day, and of those, four were operational-related. In all but two meetings through the whole week, I was asked to solve issues and give my opinion. For the first couple days, last Wednesday and Thursday, I did what I normally do: Go fast, respond, and ask very few questions. For the next two days and this morning, I made a radical switch. I did not give any answers and just asked questions. I came up with a good list:

- Tell me more about the issue.
- What is the most burning issue on this project?
- What are your reasons?
- What is the priority or priorities?
- What have you tried so far?
- What are your options?
- What are your plans going forward?
- What are you going to do differently?"

I smiled and put my hands together to feign clapping, because I was thrilled with Max's creativity. "I love the experiment. These are great questions."

"Thanks." Max seemed equally pleased.

I asked, "So how did the second half of the week go? What did you notice?"

"Two things. First, we got great results. People left meetings with clear actions to take. I definitely feel the difference between fishing and teaching to fish. Second, more than 75 percent of the issues surrounding operations or projects are 'people' related. I could not believe all the whining about 'Someone in that group over there isn't doing what they said they would do' kind of thing."

"Did you put on your coaching hat?" I asked.

"Yes, we did a lot of work on influencing: how to talk with the people who supposedly aren't doing their job, making clear requests, and how to talk with the bosses of the people who are not doing their job."

"Good going, Max."

"I also gave them a few pointers about rapport building. I told them how I've learned to slow down to match others, for instance. They got into it."

"Max, this is so great. What were people's reactions to the new you?"

"People definitely were taken aback. They were not exactly prepared when I shifted into 'question man.'"

I cracked up, then gathered myself. "Had you given them a heads-up on the experiment?"

"Not exactly; I told them after the fact. I explained that they should expect me to coach them through issues and to coach to the vision from now on. Most of them welcomed this."

"Were any of your meetings in the last week actually on the *vision roadmap?*"

"Yes. We're making progress within the team. I facilitated a team meeting this morning on the subject."

"'Facilitated,' did you?"

Max smiled. "Your lexicon is starting to creep into my vocabulary."

"Yes, we have had five months of weekly language lessons. Change cannot happen without changing language."

Max pondered a couple of moments, and asked, "Why do I sense there's a hell of a lot more behind that statement?"

"Yes, there is quite a bit of theory that would probably bore you. To use our vision-roadmap process as an example: Language is the glue that holds culture together; new visions are an example of a language change wanted or needed in an organization; and constant coaching conversations sustain the change wanted."

"So coaching conversations are like built-in reinforcements for individuals and groups?"

"Yes, coaching conversations reinforce the change you want. They are also containers for reframing."

Max nodded. "Ah, yes, we haven't talked about reframing yet."

"That brilliant list of questions you put together? Some of the questions you designed are for clarification—'to understand somebody's issue'—whether it's for problem solving, skill development, and/or career decisions. The point is that you are trying to understand the other person's perspective or what I call his or her frame."

"Frame. I got it."

"And some of those questions you designed are to help 'the person get results' or to put it more broadly—to see something new or have a different frame on a subject, right?"

"Right."

"In order for us as managers to help someone learn something new, we need to understand their frame first, in order to reframe. Otherwise we're jumping the gun, jumping to conclusions. And furthermore, the person may not be ready to hear it."

"Frame to reframe." Max hesitated. "It really does require that I totally understand where someone is coming from *before* I open my big mouth."

"Yes. You will be amazed how many gems come out of those types of conversations. Because your default is to problem solve and do a lot of telling, when you are coaching, try to focus on getting to those gems through inquiry questions instead of a constant stream of your quick opinions."

"That will be tough."

"I know. I really do." I thought to myself how hard it has been for me to master this skill. I asked Max to look at his list of questions again:

- Tell me more about the issue.
- What is the most burning issue on this project?
- What are your reasons?
- What is the priority or priorities?
- What have you tried so far?
- What are your options?
- What are your plans going forward?
- What are you going to do differently?

"You naturally put the more clarifying questions first and the more leading questions down the list. Leading questions are good when you are coaching after you have established rapport and assessed the situation. Remember RAR—rapport, assess, reframe."

Max shot back, "Believe me, I'm getting used to it."

I smiled and continued, "Leading questions do help the other person reach his or her own conclusions—which is the primary goal of coaching. Likewise, occasionally you will want to offer up a reframe outright when it will serve the other person, like I am doing with you now. This reframe can be in the form of a new word, a new behavior, or a new perspective."

"Wait, let me write this down: words, behaviors, and perspectives. Will you give me some examples?"

"No problem. Remember last session, when we were talking about coaching 'anytime, anywhere'?"

"Yeah."

"And I suggested that you look at your time differently, using the moments you do have to coach people?"

"Yeah."

"Well, in that coaching conversation, I was attempting to reframe your view of time. I offered you a new picture. You had been feeling overwhelmed with the prospect of having to coach to the new vision. My interpretation was that you saw it as one more thing to do on a never-ending list, right?"

"Yep."

"I said that coaching wouldn't take that much more time, if you leveraged your time more efficiently, both in formal one-on-ones and in between meetings. This was a reframe of your perspective."

"Ah, I get it." Max paused a moment. "That's a bit more complicated than the everyday behavior changes we have been doing—like request making and rapport building."

I nodded. "Definitely."

"OK, I get what it means to reframe perspectives and behavior. What about words?" he asked.

"Well, shifting language is actually a type of behavior. Words often jump-start us to new actions. RAR (rapport, assess, reframe) is an example; it's a distinction that helps you to remember coaching skills."

"OK."

"Reframing words can be as simple as . . . let's see . . . do you ever have a direct report come into your office and denounce a peer by saying something like: 'I'm so frustrated because the head of the so-and-so project never listens to me.'?"

"Yeah, that sounds familiar."

"What's your normal response?"

"Hmm, I would probably say something like, 'Why the heck is the project head not listening?'"

I smiled. "When someone presents a situation like this, we need to understand perceptions. Go back to the statement, 'I'm so frustrated because the head of the so-and-so project never listens to me.' Asking 'Never?' right off the bat, immediately gets the person to look at his or her own perception of the situation. It's a simple reframe with one word."

"Yeah, that would definitely get someone to think twice."

"By using certain words that are absolutes or universals, we can get into trouble because those words can perpetuate an already difficult situation. For example, 'He *always* sides with engineering,' '*Nobody* is in on that decision,' '*They* will *never* promote that guy.'"

"Jeez, I wonder how much I use those words."

"I'll let you know as I hear them!" I paused a moment, and realized we were out of time. "Max, what have you gained from this conversation that you hope to incorporate in the next couple of weeks?"

"I want to keep using my list of questions. I guess, I want to stop making it an experiment and make it a part of what I do every day."

"Great. I'll check in with you next week about how it's working."

19

Coaching Behind-the-Scenes

When Max and I sat down for our session, I asked him about the vision roadmap and to go into details about where they were in the process.

"We have met as a senior team once a week for the past three weeks, and we have aligned all of our strategies and initiatives with the new vision. Two members of our staff are putting together the communication plan for the team's review at our next staff meeting."

"That's good progress. The communication plan will include an emphasis on coaching to sustain the vision, right?"

"Yes, in fact, the team told me today that they want you to come back for two hours and help them learn to coach more consistently."

"I think you can coach them just as well as I can," I said enthusiastically.

Max nodded to signal his agreement. "I still want you to come in for a couple of hours."

"No problem."

"Now I get how important coaching is on many fronts: keeping the vision going and helping direct reports resolve issues. I coach when I sit down with them to do their yearly development plans as well."

"Yes."

"Feedback is in the coaching box, too, right?"

"Yes, it is. Coaching exists so others can learn and change, and feedback is an essential tool. How often do you give feedback to your direct reports, Max?"

"I'm pretty good about it; I usually make some comments about their projects or presentations when I have one-on-ones with them every other week."

"What about feedback right after their presentations, so it's fresh in their minds?"

"Yeah, now that I know it's cool to coach on-the-fly, I coach consciously more of the time. I was coaching just now before our meeting with one of my direct reports. I asked her to walk with me to my office."

"And you gave her feedback?"

"Yes, it was feedback I got from one of her clients that he had passed on to me. I also made a request."

"Good, often feedback is accompanied with a request for a new action." I paused for a moment, thinking back on long-term goals and some of the feedback I had gotten from Max's boss when we first started. "Remember, when we first began, one of things your boss and HR wanted you to focus on was to be less demanding and not so harsh. How have you changed this in the past five months?"

"I've definitely let up a little. I'm not so quick to be on people when we're up against a deadline."

"So you are not as critical?"

"Yeah, but I still have a long way to go."

I smiled and slowed down my pace. I wanted to get Max's attention on something deeply personal and do so without judgment. "You are critical of yourself, too, Max."

"Yeah, I'm definitely critical of myself."

"Have you let up on yourself at all?"

"Yeah, I think so. I'm trying to balance things more, be less stressed."

"Remember when we talked about the legacy work, and you said you wanted to act with more compassion?"

"Yep."

"Compassion was meant for others *and* yourself."

"Yeah, yeah." Max gave me a dismissive look. "It's hard. There are just so many things going on."

"Come on, Max. That's the trap. When in your life will you *not* say, 'There are just so many things going on'? There are an infinite number of things to do and say."

"Are you getting philosophical on me?"

"Yes, I admit, it's a path we have not taken yet. I was not trying to be too philosophical when I said that 'Compassion was meant for others *and* yourself.' You realize that you just breezed right past that."

Max smiled. "Yeah, by design."

"May I give you one reframe—another way to picture this—before we move on?"

"Yeah."

"Max, sometimes when we're overly critical of ourselves, we can more easily legitimize or rationalize being critical of others. My guess is that the more compassion you have for yourself, the more compassionate you will be of others."

"Got it."

I decided to move away from this topic because Max didn't seem like he wanted to go any further. Instead, I guided us into something related, but more practical. We hadn't addressed how he works with his peers yet, and I thought this would be a good time for that. "How are you with your peers on feedback? Do you give them feedback on a regular basis?" I asked.

"Not really. I'm not sure if any of them would want it."

"I know you appreciated getting feedback from them when you did those interviews. Wouldn't they have a similar attitude?"

"I guess."

"Giving feedback to peers is more behind-the-scenes than coaching your direct reports, which you have a license to do most of the time."

"Yeah, coaching peers is definitely different. I think it's harder."

"What is hard about it?"

"Well, first off, they are not asking for it most of the time."

I agreed and said, "Therefore, asking if they want feedback in any given moment is important. Your direct reports expect it—there is an implicit contract you have with them as their boss."

"Yeah, definitely."

"You don't have this kind of contract with your peers, so you have to make the contract explicit by agreeing to give each other feedback on an ongoing basis. Or it might just be that in any given moment you can ask, 'Are you open to some feedback right now about the last meeting?' At the same time, you must be willing to honor that they may not want your feedback."

"Yeah, that makes sense. Actually, that kind of question would be good to ask anybody."

"Exactly. People's readiness to listen is vital in terms of whether they will actually do something with the feedback. Follow-up is important, too."

Max took in the information for a few moments. "I actually have a peer that I need to talk with about something really sensitive, and I haven't figured out how to tell him yet."

"Do you want to talk about it now?" I asked.

"Yeah, it would help to strategize a bit."

"OK," I said. "Is it feedback you need to give him?"

"Sort of; I really like him but I'm hearing chatter about him from his peers in the business units."

"Did the folks in the business units tell you the information in confidence?"

"No, not exactly. It's more general. Like after a meeting, someone will complain to me as we're walking to another meeting. I keep hearing critical feedback about the

VP of marketing. But I'm not just relying on their complaints; I have witnessed some of it, too."

"So you could go to the VP of marketing without breaking confidences because you have actually observed it?"

Max nodded.

"Good, that will give you more credibility. What do you want to tell him exactly and how will you do it?" I asked.

"I think I need to talk with him casually, catch him after a meeting, and ask him if he is open to feedback. And then maybe I should have a one-on-one with him to discuss the situation in more detail."

I nodded. "That sounds like a good plan. You definitely need to ask him if he is open; by doing that you are creating an informal contract with him." I paused for a moment. "And what will you tell him?"

"He is essentially going down the wrong road in dealing with the product marketing folks. He is trying to centralize the function too much and the GMs and VPs in the line are getting pissed off. It doesn't affect me and my group, per se; I've just seen him in some meetings going after the folks in the business lines."

"OK, when you say, 'going after the folks in the business lines,' what are the observable behaviors that you see?" I asked.

"Let's see, he cuts them off a lot, and he tells them what he is planning on doing without getting their buy-in. He seems to be abusing the authority the president gave him to centralize marketing. Just because you own something, doesn't mean you just tell people what to do."

"I agree. All that does is cause resistance. So do you feel ready to give him the feedback?"

"Yeah, I feel more comfortable because I rehearsed this a bit. Thanks." Max smiled.

I made my way to the office door, turned around, and said, "Good luck in your coaching!"

FIFTH KEY

ADD THE GLOBE

Leader as Globalist

20

Breaking News

Max phoned me the day before our regular Tuesday meeting and canceled. His boss—the chief operations officer—had set up an emergency two-hour conference call that conflicted with our regular time, and there wasn't any other time that day that worked for both of us.

Max sounded surprised and was concerned that his boss was pulling in the general manager of Solano Technologies's Asia-Pacific region along with the vice president of manufacturing and IT manager there. Given the situation, Max told me that he also asked his direct report who is the IT liaison to the Asia-Pacific region to join the call.

He told me there were some major breakdowns in the IT system that were prohibiting products from being made effectively in Malaysia. Max actually was much more technical and specific than that, talking a mile a minute. I was able to decipher that there have been many application software bugs. Up until now, the bug patches had been just quick fixes; Max said, now, there needed to be an overhaul to the infrastructure. His final comment mirrored what I was thinking: "Damn, we're a high-tech company for God's sake. We should be able to do this right the first time."

Suffice it to say, Max's boss wanted a thorough analysis and asked him to plan a trip within the next two weeks to Singapore, the hub of the Asia-Pacific region. Max asked me if next week's session could be devoted entirely to preparing for his trip. "I want to talk about how I'm going to influence all the players," he said on the phone.

I agreed to that; yet after Max had revealed that he had not been anywhere in Asia, I was concerned: Influencing in Asia is very different from influencing in North America and Europe (where he had conducted business many times).

I suggested that we talk about the multiculturalism of Singapore and its business atmosphere. I told him that I've been to Singapore and many other parts of Asia, so I'll rely on that to a certain degree to support him. I also gave Max a heads-up, "There are a lot of things about the culture and business I don't know, so I'll do some research before I see you." That seemed to inspire Max to do some of his own as well.

—— 21 ——

Singapore

Max came bustling into his office. His assistant had let me in, and I was going over my notes and questions on Singapore.

Max said, "I just met with the VP of sales, who has traveled to Asia many times. Knowing that you and I were going to meet today, I was able to schedule time with him."

"Great. What did you pick up from the conversation?"

Max slowed way down and with a bit of sarcasm said, "I need to 'break bread' with my Singaporean colleagues way before I do any business."

I smiled. "Are you being sarcastic because you are surprised by his advice?"

"Well, yes, actually. I figured there would be some nuances to look out for, and at the same time, they have to be used to the way Americans do business by now. After all, Solano Technologies is a U.S.-based company."

"That's the trap, Max. They are probably used to U.S. businesspeople with their results-on-demand style; so if you do something that they are not expecting—like dine with them first—that will most likely please them."

"Yeah, the sales VP even suggested that I time my flight to arrive in the afternoon, take a quick nap, and take my colleagues out to dinner. To not even go into the office until the next day."

"A good idea. Is my assumption correct: The GM and the two other people on the conference call—the manufacturing VP and IT manager—are born somewhere in Asia? Because Singapore is very multicultural, I'm guessing that they are not all Singaporean natives."

"Yes, good guess. The GM is from Hong Kong, as is the IT manager. The manufacturing VP is from Malaysia."

"OK, then it's important to keep in mind the strong Asian virtue of 'saving face.'"

Max gave me a perplexed look. "Explain what you mean."

"Generally, it means not embarrassing another person in front of others. An example of this in Western culture is 'taking something off-line'—not to give feedback to an individual in front of his colleagues. In most Asian countries, saving face goes way beyond business. So in the case of dinner, because you are the guest of the country, the GM will probably insist on treating you to an exquisite dinner, and would be offended if you paid—you need to save face with him."

"OK, that's easy enough."

"Max, try to pull out all your compassionate gracious genes for this trip. Things are more formal there, and much more traditional. They don't have the beer-football thing going on."

"Are you suggesting I'm going to be an ugly American?"

I smiled and squinted a bit, hoping I did not offend Max. "No, I'm sorry, did I just lose face with you?"

Max smiled. "No, just kidding."

"I was kidding, too." I paused for a moment and thought about the last time I traveled to Asia. "Max, by the way: 'kidding around' is one thing that's going to be hard there. When I have traveled in Asia, my humor and wit did not work so well. One time, I was trying to convey the importance of the 'whole' organizational system in doing strategic planning. I was teaching a leadership workshop in Singapore with participants from Malaysian, Indian, and Chinese backgrounds. I used the metaphor 'whole enchilada' as a way to explain the concept. That was a dumb move. Thankfully, I stopped myself, and asked if anyone even knew what an enchilada was, much less the expression."

"Whole enchilada. That's pretty funny and . . . bad."

"Yes, it was one of those defining moments for me early in my career: I vowed I would watch my American English slang and idioms. Many Asian businesspeople have been raised learning two languages—English and their native tongue. But in most cases, the English is of the British variety, so even if participants have been raised with English, American slang does not work."

"I guess small talk is going to take on a whole new meaning. I have my work cut out for me."

"If you prepare a little, you will be fine. Does the sales VP know the people you are meeting with?"

"Yeah, he gave me the rundown on each of them as far as their idiosyncrasies. I know the Asia-Pacific IT manager, of course, but only through phone calls. He is dotted line to me and is solid-line reporting to the manufacturing VP. He told me all of them have families. I guess that should be the basis of our small talk."

"Good idea. Do you want to hear another suggestion?"

"I'm all ears."

I laughed out loud. "Sorry, I was having a little chuckle to myself. I just got this image of you saying 'I'm all ears' in Singapore, and the look of confusion you might get."

"Don't worry."

"I'm not, really. But I am looking forward to hearing about the things that get lost in translation. You will make some mistakes, and that's OK. The key is catching yourself."

"Yeah, it should be interesting." Max paused. "So, what was your suggestion?"

"Oh, thanks for tracking there, Max. That part of you that you are working on—that compassionate mentor, the one who wants to slow down—you will want to focus on this. I predict you will learn to listen on this trip like you never have before."

"What do you mean?"

"First, just practically, you will have to slow down your processing and concentrate more because of the accents; and second, don't assume anything. Things such as the idea of goal setting and strategic planning are not the same there, as a general rule. Neither are agreements."

"OK, say more. You got me intrigued."

"You know, sometimes with an employee, when you request something, you both agree to it and then the person does not get it done. Generally, this is a function of people wanting to please you in the agreement, so they say yes, even though they can't or won't do what they say. This phenomenon is more pronounced in places like Singapore, Japan, China, and Hong Kong."

"So what do I do about agreements? We're going to have to make some agreements in order to get the systems overhauled." Max put his hands out in front of him to get my attention. "Of course, this is after we have all eaten a lot and listened a lot."

"Good, I'm glad you are catching on. I hope your sarcasm does not seep out over there."

"No, really. How should I approach getting agreements made?" Max asked.

"Let's go through it on a high level first, OK? I need a lot more information." I paused for a moment. "Tell me more about the problem first. You said on the phone that the system needs to be overhauled, right?"

"Yes, let me give you a little history. You should know my direct report—the liaison to the Asia-Pacific region—and the IT manager in Singapore have been working on the system overhaul for a while now. You see, Asia-

Pac's manufacturing plant uses different supply chain software and networking gear than we do here in Silicon Valley's plant. We have updated as much as we can and have patched where we can. But there are still lots of problems with compatibility."

"I'm curious why there was a different infrastructure and software applications in the first place."

"Good point. Three years ago, Solano acquired the arm of a big company that was based in Singapore. That company was on totally different systems at the time of the acquisition, and we decided to wait to change the infrastructure until a quarter ago. Because the manufacturing had doubled since the acquisition, we thought it was time to do the infrastructure overhaul."

"OK, I'm following."

"So back in November, I asked the Asia-Pac IT liaison, who is based here, and the IT manager in Singapore to work on the infrastructure overhaul. The planning and project management is not going well; that's why my boss jumped in to call a meeting. He received a call directly from the Asia-Pac GM."

"What's the root of the problem from the GM's perspective?"

"Mostly, it boils down to everyone wants better productivity, but they don't agree that a complete overhaul is the answer. They think we want the overhaul just so that they can become compatible with our system."

"Is that true?"

"No, no. We think this is the best system for them to go on; otherwise, they will max out on production."

"So you are dealing with and will continue to deal with a lot of resistance."

"Yep, even more reason why I should go over there and just listen, right?"

I nodded vigorously. "How effective has your Asia-Pac liaison been at listening?"

"Horrible, apparently, which I didn't know until last week's conference call. The GM did not want him on the call. I knew the project was hard for him, and I was giving him coaching along the way, but not much was working, apparently."

"Has he been over there at all?"

Max shook his head. "No, he hasn't."

I gave Max a look of confusion.

"I know, I know, he is the Asia-Pac liaison after all, which, by the way, is not his only job within IT. Nevertheless, you would think he would have traveled over there at some point. I think he took the 'save money' principle we have around here too seriously."

I nodded. "Yeah, a person with a worldwide view—or what I call a globalist—knows when to be virtual and use the phone and e-mail, and when *not* to be virtual and jump on a plane."

Max hesitated a moment, then said, "Yeah, good point; he hasn't figured out the difference."

"I have another question: Did the Asia-Pac GM ask you to come over there or did your boss?"

"I guess they both agreed to it when they talked originally."

"What else transpired during the conference call last week?"

"The main thing is that the GM is not willing to sacrifice his numbers—productivity numbers—to overhaul the infrastructure. That's what the GM is paid on, and he would not take the COO's guarantee that we as a company are OK with the shutdown—that's what it's going to take to do the overhaul. I think our president will need to get involved eventually, but in the meantime, our COO wants me to go over and learn all the details of the infrastructure plan and the ramifications to his plant."

"So you are going on a discovery mission, of sorts?" I asked.

Max looked frustrated. "Yes, because apparently our liaison has not discovered enough already."

"Are you going to take him with you?"

"That's a good question. I'm debating that. Half of me wants to fire him and half of me wants him to get it, and learn from his mistakes. I guess the other option is just to leave him here, and deal with him when I get back. Got any advice?"

"What principles are you going to use to make the decision?"

Max responded, "The main thing to figure out is if the relationships with the GM and the manufacturing VP are salvageable assuming the present Asia-Pac liaison remains."

"How much was he really dealing with the GM and the manufacturing VP? From what you have said so far, it sounds like the liaison dealt mostly with the IT manager there."

"Yeah, that's partly true. He actually deals with all of them." Max paused to think. "I don't want to fire him; he does a good job in other areas; he is a major producer. Gets a lot of things done; he is just a little rough around the edges."

"Gee, Max, that sounds like someone else I know from six months ago."

"Yeah, I know. It's occurred to me that he reminds me of myself. That's part of why I want to give him a break, coach him a little, and see how he takes to it."

"I think that's a great option, assuming it's also best for the company."

"That's no question, because he's been here four years and already knows a lot about the company and the industry."

"So, then, are you leaning toward taking him with you?"

"Yeah, I think I am now. I'm going to have him do some studying before we leave, though. And we can fly over together so we can get our ducks in a row."

"Sounds like a good plan." I paused. "May I give you a list of ideas to help your studying?"

"Yes."

"First, I recommend that you do some research on key business and industry trends there *and* on cultural/religious norms for Singapore, Hong Kong, China, and Malaysia."

"That seems like a lot in one week."

"That's why I want to help you. I can ask my researcher to do the big-picture work, and you and the Asia-Pac liaison can focus on interviewing people in Solano who know your colleagues in Singapore. Your new guy from Vancouver, his parents are from Hong Kong, right?"

"Yeah, they are. I'll start with him," Max said.

"Good idea. Also, I have a good coaching tool that you may share with the Asia-Pac liaison. It's a general guideline to being a globalist, and you can use it to jump-start your conversation with him about what mistakes he has made and the goals for moving forward."

Globalists are wise and effective leaders who:

Know they do not exist in a vacuum and understand context and systems.

Incorporate a global perspective in setting a strategic direction.

Understand cultural differences at home and away.

Know when to be virtual and when not to be.

Max said, "I wish I would have looked at this three months ago, and used it in my meetings with him."

"What will you emphasize with him first, now?"

"What you said earlier today about when to be virtual and when not to be is key to influencing him to go with me. And for now, we want to understand as much as possible about the cultural differences. I realize now, I should have been taking him and my Singaporean colleagues into account more in my strategic plan."

I nodded. "Based on what you just said, may I give you a coaching tip?"

"Yeah, of course."

"When you are talking with him about cultural differences, or any of the guidelines for that matter, remember that you are coaching—understand his frame first, before you reframe."

"Good reminder." Max paused and looked at the list again. "Tell me more about the first point. Give me an example."

"The idea, 'Globalists know they do not exist in a vacuum and understand context and systems,' is about having a big-picture view. We often associate this with having a worldview, but it does not have to be about a world matter. For you, it could be ensuring that your vision aligns with the company's. It's also the antidote to silos: Don't get stuck in your own views, protecting your own team. When I asked you earlier, 'Is it best for the company to take the Asia-Pac liaison with you?' I was putting things in context."

"OK, it's about the big picture. Easy to believe, harder to do. A lot of us are stuck in our silos protecting our turf."

"Yes, some executives are afraid of losing what they have."

Max interrupted me, "That's a controversial topic we will save for another day. Anything else to prepare me for my trip?"

I smiled. "What publications do you read on a regular basis?"

Max thought for a moment. "I read *Fortune* and the *Harvard Business Review.*"

"Those are good, generally. I suggest you read the following to prepare for this trip: *The Economist, Far Eastern Economic Review,* and the *Asian Wall Street Journal.* You will have lots of time on the plane."

"OK, I'll pick those up at the airport."

"I also want to backtrack to our earlier conversation about agreements. I think it's a good idea to stay in the discovery mode as much as possible, and take back info to the company's president. Because the GM reports to him, the two of them will make the final agreement. Try to get a sense of how important rank is to the GM."

"Yeah, that's a good idea and pretty much what my boss told me."

"One more thing: I did not realize until I looked carefully this morning that next week's meeting is supposed to be the last one of our six-month contract. Because you are leaving on Wednesday, I thought we should meet on Tuesday to review your accomplishments and talk about the next steps. Are you game for that?"

"Wow, it's already six months. Unbelievable. Yeah, let's do it."

"OK, good luck in preparing for Singapore."

"See you next Tuesday."

CHAPTER

22

Becoming a Corporate Sage

When I arrived in Max's office, he looked frazzled.

"Are you excited to go on your trip or just plain frantic?" I asked.

"Both," he said with a big smile.

I laughed out loud, and before I had a chance to ask another question, he added some details. "Because I'll be gone a week, there are a few things I need to tidy up before I leave, including the vision roadmap work. I asked two of my directors—including the new hire from Vancouver—to finish that up."

"Good, glad you are delegating. By the way, were you able to talk with your new director about Chinese culture? I remember you saying last week that he was top on your list."

"Yep, I met with him last Wednesday. It was a good meeting."

"Did he offer any tips?" I asked.

"He definitely backed up what you said about 'breaking bread'—although he didn't call it that. He gave me insight into hierarchy and honor and told me how it's different from our American brand of hierarchy, which is normally associated with power. Because my level is one down from the GM's there, I'll definitely need to report my findings to our CEO and let them come to an agreement."

"Good, I'm grateful that what we discussed last week was on the right track, and that the new director confirmed much of what we talked about."

Max continued. "The other good thing he did was agree to coach the Asia-Pac liaison before we leave, and to continue when we get back."

"That's great!"

"I also have had two meetings with the Asia-Pac liaison. I've listened a lot to his frustrations, and we brainstormed our approach to the discovery process in Singapore. He really appreciated the globalist guidelines you gave me last week, and we talked about examples he can put to use right away."

"Max, it sounds like you have learned a lot and coached a lot in the last week."

"Yeah, and this is where I want to start as far as my six-month accomplishments. We were going to spend some time on that today, right?"

I immediately responded, "Yes, go for it."

"I'm really happy with how I have coached the Asia-Pac liaison, and I hope our talks will make a difference for him on our trip. One of my original goals was to improve communication with my direct reports, and I hope we can count this as a success story upon our return."

I nodded. "Yes, I'll be curious how things are mended while you and he are there." I looked down at the notes I had prepared for today and said, "Let's look back at the original agreement letter; the three focus areas were: (1) better communications with team, (2) be more strategic and influential with peers, and (3) be less stressed and less demanding. So what are some accomplishments surrounding communication with your team you want to highlight?"

"Well, I feel like I've come full circle. I mean, six months ago, I was the one bowling people over with my style. Now, I'm doing it less and noticing it a lot more in other people. I'm much more tuned in to how my behavior affects others."

"Yes, I think you are more tuned in to how your emotions affect others, too." I added.

"You call that emotional intelligence, right?"

I nodded.

"Would you also put this in the category my boss wanted me to work on—executive presence?" Max asked.

I nodded again and said, "Yes, being more aware of the effect of your behavior and emotions fits into probably any category or focus area. It's definitely at the core of being a great leader. How do you think it has particularly helped you in communication with your team?"

"Mainly, I think, I let them participate more in meetings. I don't interrupt them as much. I still have a way to go, though. I've not perfected this by any means."

"Max, there's always something more to learn—and I truly mean always—which can feel burdensome after a while. That's why it's so important to survey accomplishments every so often, to realize how far you have come."

"Yeah, I agree."

"What else have you noticed about communication with your team?" I asked.

"The sessions on how-to-coach have really helped me. I definitely find more opportunities to coach in-the-moment, and I'm listening better. I would rate myself a B– in this skill. It's going to take a long time to become good at this."

I smiled, knowing full well how right he is; becoming good at coaching does take a long time. "Max, you are a better coach now than you were six months ago, and you are going to be an even better coach a year from now." I paused to settle on a new question. "What about practices on the Communication Checklist? How would you rate yourself against this?"

"You mean on skills like meeting management and request making?"

"Yes, those are two on the list."

"Those are the two I've mastered. Our meetings are definitely more consistent and effective. They actually start and end on time now. And making requests is now a habit for me; others are catching on, too."

"Let's talk about the next steps regarding communication with your team: Are there skills you want to focus on in the next three months that you weren't able to concentrate on in the past six months?"

Max pondered the question a moment. "I want to delegate more, and particularly I want to name someone the COO of the IT organization, so he or she is running more of the day-to-day. And I want to use my time to coach that person."

"Yes, I remember that you had mentioned the importance of having a right-hand person. I think this is a good idea, especially if you're willing to take the time to coach him or her." I looked back down on my list. "Let's talk about strategy—what inroads have you made there?"

"The obvious accomplishment is the vision roadmap. But it's more than that. I'm thinking differently about strategy now—that it needs to be part of everyday work, not some one-time planning session. I'm much more strategic in my conversations with my peers, too, both formally and informally. I think in the next year this is going to be the hardest thing to do—to keep a long-term and broad view. Given the constant fire drills around here, it's easier to stay tactical."

"Max, I want to point out that the shift in how you look at strategy coupled with the vision roadmap and the fact you want to hire a COO means you have the beginnings of your organizational legacy. This is tough to do in six months, and you have an excellent start. I guess I'm especially happy about this accomplishment because of its long-lasting effect on you and others."

"Are you getting sentimental on me?" Max blurted out.

"And if I were? What's the matter with that?"

It was as if Max realized in that very moment that this could be our last meeting. He slowed down his tempo and said, "I suppose nothing."

I contemplated the idea that this could be our last meeting and became a little sad. I liked Max a lot for many reasons, mostly because we both really understood each other with full acceptance. I paused a moment longer to determine what to ask next.

"Max, what about the other part of this focus area—influencing peers?"

"No doubt, the number one accomplishment here is those interviews you made me do."

"You know, the hair on the back of my neck stands up when you say that I made you do something."

Max chuckled. "I know you hate that, but it's sort of true. I mean, I would have never initiated those interviews on my own unless you strongly encouraged me to do so."

"Yes, I know that made a big difference to you and to the people you talked with. What skills did you get out of those interviews?"

"Practicing small talk and getting into rapport, asking good questions, listening. This led to understanding the interviewees better."

"Which led to?"

"Mostly it led to having a better relationship with each of them. It's so much easier now to interact with each of them in meetings."

"Great. Now, when you return from Singapore, are you willing to go back to those same interviewees and ask them the same questions in order to get some feedback on your progress?"

"So our discussion here won't suffice?" Max asked.

"Actually, this discussion will suffice for fulfilling my obligations to your boss and HR. I think going back to the original interviewees will be both rewarding for you and them and deepen your learning a lot." I smiled and took a conscious breath. "I'm in this for your learning."

"Got it, and thank you. I think what makes sense is for my assistant to set those meetings for a couple weeks after I get back."

"Another goal you had was to be less stressed and less demanding. How does that look to you now?"

"Very different from when we started. The breathing helped, the personal legacy work helped. I'm spending less time here and more time with my family in the evenings."

I asked, "And your wife and son have noticed?"

"Yes, they have told me."

"Good." I paused. "You know, Max, I think you have more compassion for yourself now."

"Sometimes it's hard for me to admit that, but, yeah, I really think I'm more patient now with myself and others. And this I truly will be working on the rest of my life."

"I'm not going to disagree with you on that. At the same time, you are well on your way to becoming a corporate sage."

"I do like the idea that I discovered some wisdom in this tired body of mine," Max said.

"You really did, and that newfound wisdom is going to come in handy in Singapore."

"I hope so. I'll call you when I return, and we can talk about continuing our coaching together. I'm going to talk with my boss about it, too, when I get back."

"That makes sense, because when you are gone, I'll send your boss and the HR VP a copy of your accomplishments."

"Great."

"Max, may I leave you with a little something you can recite to yourself during those moments of frustration, on this trip and when you get back?"

"Yeah, that would be nice."

"This is called a 'metta' meditation. *Metta* is the Sanskrit word for compassion.'"

Before I read it aloud to him, I wrote this passage in his notebook so he would have it on his trip:

> May you be happy
> May you be safe
> May you be healthy
> May you live with ease
> May you be free

A

Skills and Tools Reference List

You will find these on the pages listed. Find the books in the Bibliography.

- Request making—7, 20. For more information, read *Smart Work* and *Understanding Computers and Cognition*.
- Responding to requests—20.
- Interview feedback questions—36.
- Small talk questions—52.
- Rapport building—57. For more information, read *Smart Work*.
- Balancing inquiry and advocacy—70. For more information, read *The Fifth Discipline Fieldbook*.
- Communication Checklist—88.
- Personal legacy questions—109.
- Team legacy questions—five-for-the-future—126–27.
- Shared vision questions—128.

- **ITM** Coaching Model—148-49. For more information, read *ITM Coaching in Action: What, When, and How of Coaching in Interrupt-Driven Cultures.*
- Globalist guidelines—182. For more information, read *The Lexus and the Olive Tree.*

Visit http://www.corporatesage.com to learn more about being a corporate sage.

— B —

Corporate Sage Leadership Skills Questions

The Corporate Sage Leadership Framework consists of five key roles that parallel the five parts of the book:

Leader as Learner

Leader as Relationship Builder

Leader as Visionary

Leader as Coach

Leader as Globalist

Ask yourself the questions Max's coach asks him!

- What behaviors and/or leadership habits do you want to change?
- What cues remind you to slow down and put conscious attention on these desired changes?
- What *gearshift* (1 to 5) do you run at during a typical workday? How does modulating your speed for different relationships and situations contribute to your effectiveness?
- What destructive emotions sometimes prevent you from getting what you want or getting things done?
- Do other people experience you as empathetic because you slow down to listen to them and seek to understand their emotional state and situation?
- Using the *Who? What? When?* questions, how can you be more effective and clear with your everyday requests?
  - Who?—Who is the request directed to? In other words, who owns the action?
  - What?—What are the specific conditions that need to be in place so you will be satisfied with the results?
  - When?—What is the time attached to the request? When is it due?

Get Good at Small Talk
(Leader as Relationship Builder)

- Most likely, you have climbed the ladder of success by being results-driven. As you move up the ranks, building relationships becomes even more important. How do you put more attention on building your *relationship network* outside of your reporting structure?

- How do you rate your *small talk* skills? What *signature* questions could you access in informal and formal conversations?

- Do you put attention on *matching* others' behavior (tone, tempo, body language, words) in order to be in rapport?

- How well do you *balance inquiry and advocacy* when you are influencing someone? What does it take for you to make adjustments in-the-moment?

- What is your *influenceable factor*? In other words, how open are you to being influenced?

Craft a Legacy with Great People + Vision
(Leader as Visionary)

- When you have an opening on your team, instead of filling a gap immediately, do you ask yourself: "What great people are out there that I need to have on my team?"

- How much time do you spend on *strategic planning* per month? What about *strategic thinking*—do you think strategically, and take in the long view, in some fashion every day?

- Before you begin the process of establishing a team or organizational legacy, ask yourself the *personal legacy* questions:
  - Values—What do you consider to be five of the most important values that you live by?
  - Gift—What do you think your greatest gift (or skill) is as a leader?
  - Known for—When coworkers think of you, what are you most known for now?
  - Possible shifts—What do want to be known for now that you are not yet known for?
  - Known for in the future—Imagine that I (your coach) was having a conversation with one of your friends 20 years from now. What would you want that person to say about you?
- In order to think "outside the box" ask your team the *five-for-the-future* questions:
  - Five years from now, what do you see the world being like (consider economy, politics, health, society, etc.)?
  - Five years from now, how will technology affect global business?
  - Five years from now, how will your company contribute to global business?
  - Five years from now, how will your team/organization influence the industry in which you are in?

- Five years from now, how will your team/organization influence your company, overall, as a business?

Coach In-the-Moment to Build a Legacy (Leader as Coach)

- How well do you leverage hallway conversations to guide people on your team and give them feedback?
- When you coach one-to-one, how regularly do you use the **ITM** Coaching skills: *rapport, assess, reframe?*
- Do you consciously use coaching to sustain change management programs/projects?

Add the Globe (Leader as Globalist)

- How do you keep yourself updated on global financial markets so you can anticipate and prepare for their impact on your industry and company?
- How often are you reading business and industry-related magazines? How many of those are non–U.S. published?
- How do you learn about the cultural and business customs of the countries that you are doing business with?
- How do you determine when to be virtual and when not to be, when working with colleagues in other locations?

Bibliography

Albom, Mitch. *Tuesdays with Morrie*. New York: Doubleday Books, 1997.

Bethanis, Susan J. "Language as Action: Linking Metaphors with Organization Transformation." In *Learning Organizations: Developing Cultures for Tomorrow's Workplace*, Sarita Chawla and John Renesch, eds. Portland, Ore.: Productivity Press, Inc., 1995.

Bethanis, Susan J., and Thuy H. Sindell. *ITM Coaching in Action: What, When, and How to Coach in Interrupt-Driven Cultures*. See http://www.mariposaleadership.com/resources.html.

Cialdini, Robert. "Harnessing the science of persuasion." *Harvard Business Review* (October 2001).

Collins, Jim. *Good to Great*. New York: Harper Collins, 2001.

Conger, Jay. "The necessary art of persuasion." *Harvard Business Review* (May–June 1998).

Eisler, Riane. *The Chalice and the Blade*. San Francisco: Harper Books, 1987.

Flaherty, James. *Coaching: Evoking Excellence in Others*. Burlington, Mass.: Elsevier, 1999.

Friedman, Thomas. L. *The Lexus and the Olive Tree*. New York: Farrar, Straus, Giroux, 1999.

——. *Longitudes and Attitudes: Exploring the World after September 11*. New York: Farrar, Straus, Giroux, 2002.

Garten, Jeffrey. *The Mind of the CEO*. New York: Basic Books, 2001.

Giuliani, Rudolph. *Leadership*. New York: Hyperion, 2002.

Goleman, Daniel. "What makes a leader?" *Harvard Business Review* (November–December 1998).

Goleman, Daniel, Richard Boyatzis, and Annie McKee. *Primal Leadership: Realizing the Power of Emotional Intelligence*. Boston: Harvard Business School Publishing, 2002.

Hamel, Gary. "Strategy as revolution." *Harvard Business Review* (July–August 1996).

Heidegger, Martin. *On the Way to Language*. New York: Harper & Row, 1982.

Kouzes, James M., and Barry Z. Posner. *The Leadership Challenge: How to Keep Getting Extraordinary Things Done in Organizations*. San Francisco: Jossey-Bass, 1995.

Lakoff, George, and Mark Johnson. *Metaphors We Live By.* 2d ed. Chicago: University of Chicago Press, 2003.

Lencioni, Patrick. *The Five Temptations of a CEO: A Leadership Fable.* San Francisco: Jossey-Bass, 1998.

Marshall, Lisa, and Lucy Freedman. *Smart Work: The Syntax Guide for Mutual Understanding in the Workplace.* Dubuque, Iowa: Kendall-Hunt, 1995.

Morgan, Gareth. *Images of Organization.* 2nd ed. Thousand Oaks, Calif.: Sage Publications, 1997.

Nhāt Hanh, Thích. *The Miracle of Mindfulness.* Boston: Beacon Press, 1976.

Nisker, Wes. *Buddha's Nature: Evolution as a Practical Guide to Enlightenment.* New York: Bantam Books, 1998.

Richmond, Lewis. *Work as a Spiritual Practice.* New York: Broadway Books, 1999.

Senge, Peter M., et al. *The Fifth Discipline Fieldbook: Strategies and Tools for Building a Learning Organization.* New York: Doubleday, 1994.

Sontag, Susan. *Illness as Metaphor.* Toronto: Collins Publishers, 1978.

Whitwoth, Laura, Henry Kimsey-House, and Phil Sandahl. *Co-Active Coaching: New Skills for Coaching People Toward Success in Work and Life.* Palo Alto, Calif.: Davies-Black Publishing, 1998.

Winograd, Terry, and Fernando Flores. *Understanding Computers and Cognition.* Norwood, N.J.: Ablex Publishing, 1986.